Deciding to Be
Christian

A DAILY COMMITMENT

Mark O'Keefe, OSB

Liguori
LIGUORI, MISSOURI

Imprimi Potest:
Harry Grile, CSsR, Provincial
Denver Province, The Redemptorists

Published by Liguori Publications
Liguori, Missouri 63057

To order, call 800-325-9521, or visit liguori.org.

Library of Congress Cataloging-in-Publication Data

O'Keefe, Mark, 1956-
  Deciding to be Christian : a daily commitment / Mark O'Keefe.—1st ed.
    p. cm.
  ISBN 978-0-7648-2118-9
  1. Christian life—Catholic authors. 2. Conversion—Catholic Church. I. Title.
  BX2350.3.O42 2011
  248.4'82—dc23
                        2011046467

Liguori Publications, a nonprofit corporation, is an apostolate of the Redemptorists. To learn more about the Redemptorists, visit Redemptorists.com.

Printed in the United States of America
16 15 14 13 12 / 5 4 3 2 1
First Edition

Contents

INTRODUCTION

Decisions. We make dozens, maybe hundreds of them each day. A few are important and deserving of careful forethought: Should I change jobs? Should I withhold or share this important information with a friend? Most of them are insignificant: This shirt or that one? Wheat bread or rye? One more hour of television or off to bed early?

Our lives are full of decisions. Although we may not often think about it, the Christian life also is a decision, a life commitment. It is lived out in a series of daily decisions. In order to truly be a Christian—in order to authentically, maturely, and fully live the Christian life—we must *decide* to be Christian, and we must renew that decision each day. There is no other way.

Yes, many of us were baptized as infants, and, in that sense, we have been Christians our whole lives. It is also true that baptism is a sacrament in which Christ works, marking us permanently, uniting us with Christ at the core of our being. Yet at the same time we all know there is a difference between being a Christian "in name" and living as a Christian in reality. There's a difference between having been transformed interiorly in Christ and actually living out that transformation in our daily living while both deepening it and broadening its scope in our lives. There's a difference between continuing the formalities or externals of a religion and truly believing, embracing, and living a faith. And that difference is *decision*—a life decision and daily decision. If we have been baptized as infants, we must decide to embrace our new life in Christ daily live its demands. We must decide to be truly a disciple of Jesus Christ in our daily lives and relationships: a Christian more than in name only or in occasional, halfhearted practice.

I have been privileged to teach moral theology for many years, a discipline that focuses on the shape and demands of Christian discipleship. I have pondered and taught, many times over, about decision-making—shoulds, oughts, rules, norms. But it is my experience as a pastor for these last few years that has focused my reflections on the utter necessity of the life decision to be a Christian and of making all of our other decisions based on this fundamental and all-encompassing life commitment.

Each Sunday, as a pastor, I rise to preach the Good News to a congregation of people, some of whom have fully embraced and live their Christian faith wholeheartedly each day. There are others who sincerely want to live a Christian life without a sense that this requires a deepening of faith and a growing integration of the entirety of their lives around their faith. But it seems to me that I am preaching to many others who are not exactly sure why they still go to Mass (whether regularly, occasionally, or from time to time) or what difference their faith might make beyond the doors of the church. Surely this variety in depth of understanding and commitment is nothing new in Christian history, but, in my experience and judgment, this last group of the marginally committed grows generation by generation, year by year. The Church's response, as Pope John Paul II taught so forcefully, is evangelization. Our response, as individuals, is our own personal decision and commitment within the life of the wider community of faith.

What I offer in *Deciding to Be Christian* is a reflection on the Christian life and its foundational commitment—its shape, scope, demands, unfolding, obstacles, supports, context, and goals. It is a reflection based on pastoral observations and experience, academic training and teaching, and my own experience as a Christian on our shared journey. But, at another level, what I offer here is a sustained exhortation to take with utter seriousness the Christian commitment in its totality. It is for that reason that, although each chapter could be read independently, one is encouraged to read through the book as a whole as it tries to unfold the broader picture that will make sense of it parts.

Roman Catholic understanding forms definitively this vision of the shape and the landscape of the Christian life. But at the same time, the basic decision and commitment that is reflected here is the common, foundational baptismal commitment of all of those who take seriously the invitation of Jesus to follow him. These reflections are offered to those who feel ready to embrace their Christian faith more vigorously or who at least want to know what such a commitment might mean and how to embrace it. They are offered to both individuals and groups for reflection and discussion. And, although *Deciding to Be Christian* is not a textbook of moral theology, both those in moral theology and students of moral theology will discover a vision of the Christian life that this discipline seeks to support, shape, and further. The profound truth of our moral and spiritual tradition and the riches of the Church's moral teaching will fall on deaf ears in our contemporary world if we have not thought carefully and thoroughly about the real people with whom we want to share it, the actual context in which they live their faith (or not) today, and the challenges that we face in our dialogue with them.

My deepest gratitude goes to Dr. Tom and Rita Walters and to Father Larry Richardt, who read drafts of the book and offered helpful comments and challenges, and to Jane Wendholt, who carefully proofread the text. I owe a deep debt of gratitude to my dear friends, Nancy and Ray Larkin.

Deciding to Be Christian is dedicated to the people of St. Mary's Catholic Church in Huntingburg, Indiana, where I am privileged to serve as pastor.

Questions for Reflection

* *Were there particular moments or periods in your life when you feel that you made an adult decision to claim and live your faith more deeply?*

* *At this moment, how do you view the depth and solidity of your commitment as a Christian? How might you make it stronger?*

* *How do your everyday decisions manifest, strengthen, or weaken your commitment as a Christian?*

* *Do you know other Christians who seem to have a firm Christian commitment or life of faith that you would like to emulate? What about them makes them seem like more solid Christians?*

Prayer

Loving God, you have graciously called me to Christian faith, and you are always inviting me into a deeper friendship with you. Renew and reenliven now that gift of faith. Help me to accept your invitation more completely and to decide once again, today and every day, even more strongly, to embrace Christ and his way of living. This I pray in the name of the same Christ our Lord. Amen.

DECIDING TO BE CHRISTIAN

S ome decades ago, theologian Karl Rahner rather famously said that, in the future, the Christian will be a mystic or he or she won't exist. He used "mystic" not to refer to extraordinary spiritual experience; rather, he was speaking of a real experience of God that comes from the heart of our existence. Thus, to say it another way, the future Christian will decide to be Christian because he or she has a concrete and deep experience with God. The future is now. The days are past when we can expect most people to remain Christian simply out of custom, societal, or family pressure, or because of a dry conceptual acceptance of doctrine. In our day, if we are truly Christians, it is because we have decided to be, based on some personal experience of God's presence and invitation to us.

As the title of this book suggests, each of us must personally decide to be Christian. Whether baptized as infants or not, at some point, if we are truly to be and to remain Christian in anything more than name and superficial observance, we must each make an adult decision. Of course, it is true that faith is always a divine gift and invitation. God is always the one who takes the initiative. God's grace is always the principal agent in our acceptance of faith and our growth at every step along the way. But the point here is that it is no longer possible (if it ever was) simply to be born into the faith and assume that one will eventually choose to live as a Christian. In our time and in our society as it is, we must each decide to live as Christians and view ourselves and our world as Christians do.

A truly Catholic vision has always understood the Church to be a large and inclusive reality. We do not understand ourselves to be a "sect," a group of the special "elect." There have always been and will always be Catholics with varying levels of understanding, commitment, and adherence. This is not to try to define the essential elements of what makes someone "Catholic." Nor is it to suggest that those who consciously and firmly decide to be Christian thereby make themselves the arbiters of who is or is not a "true" Catholic or

Christian. Jesus, even as he invited others to follow him, consistently and clearly condemned any judgment of others (Matthew 7:1–5). Who, after all, can judge the heart and commitment of anyone else, especially when it is so hard to judge our own? Who can really say that his own commitment is deep enough or his commitment firm enough to permit a smug and self-satisfied contentment? With God's help and mercy, we each humbly make our own commitment as best we can. As for the commitment of others, we can let God sort all of that out and pray that our faith will grow stronger and that other Catholics will come to their own mature and adult decisions about the faith and how they will live it. We must decide for ourselves to be Christian and to embrace the rest of the Christian community, drawing life from the Spirit always present in the Church as it is and contributing in our own way to the life of the body of Christ and to the faith of our brothers and sisters.

To speak of a basic Christian decision is not to propose that there can be any kind of a measuring stick of who should or should not be counted as a Christian and as a "true" member of the Church. Yet, Christian discipleship was never meant to be halfhearted, part-time, or lukewarm: "I know your works; you are neither cold nor hot. I wish that you were either cold or hot. So, because you are lukewarm, and neither cold nor hot, I am about to spit you out of my mouth" (Revelation 3:15–16).

The Gospels make this point quite evident. Jesus was clear, unequivocal, and frequent about the commitment demanded of his disciples: "Whoever loves father or mother more than me is not worthy of me; and whoever loves son or daughter more than me is not worthy of me; and whoever does not take up the cross and fol-low after me is not worthy of me. Those who find their life will lose it, and those who lose their life for my sake will find it" (Matthew 10:37–39; see also Matthew 16:24–25, Mark 8:34–35, Luke 9:23–24 and 14:26–27, and John 12:25–26). Recall also how Jesus challenged the rich young man: "You lack one thing; go, sell what you own, and give the money to the poor, and you will have treasure in heaven; then come, follow me" (Mark 10:21; see also Matthew 19:21 and Luke 18:22).

Was Jesus exaggerating? Did he not intend to be taken seriously? In fact, even acknowledging that these texts must be understood critically and in context, it is abundantly clear that the disciples of Jesus were meant to stand firmly on the rock that is Christ, without trying to straddle that true rock and the sandy ground of secular values and ideas. Yes, we live "in the world." Yes, there is good in the world around us, upon which we depend. Yes, it is true that there is no pure life of the Spirit that exists in this life, separate from ordinary daily life. Yes...but...

Our Christian faith is a faith in the God-made-flesh who died on the cross. It is the faith for which countless martyrs shed their lifeblood and upon which an endless number of Christians have staked their lives. It is the faith that has supported and challenged, consoled and inflamed men and women of every state in life, in every age—not just courageous martyrs in times of active persecution, not just monks and nuns living in cloisters, or hermits living out in the wilderness, but *ordinary* men and women living ordinary lives but precisely and decisively as Christians.

Those of us who would truly be Christians cannot settle for some watered-down version of Christianity—"Christianity-*lite*." I am not suggesting that every Christian is called to go out into the desert to live the solitary life of the hermit or into the cloister or out to the foreign missions. Perhaps for many ages in the life of the Church, it was believed that the seriousness of Jesus' challenge was intended for some special group of "heroic" disciples. But this is simply not true. In fact, it is an excuse for not embracing the Gospel challenge of Jesus that was clearly not intended for a few but rather for all. Yes, we will all live the Christian commitment differently according to our particular circumstances and our state in life. But the simple fact is that every Christian must personally decide to live the Christian life and its demands fully and completely, whether as a married person, parent, widow, single person, vowed religious, priest, or any person desiring to follow Christ.

And that means decision. In fact, it means a daily-renewed decision. It means that we get up in the morning and renew our commitments, with the help of God, to be a Christian today. When we fall or fail, we ask for pardon and then, with God's help, get back up and renew our commitments.

"Christian" must be who and what we are. Being Christian, being a disciple of Jesus Christ, must be at the very core of our identities. Who are you? I am a Christian! I am not only a father or a wife or an attorney or a manager who happens also to be a Christian. No, I am a *Christian* father, a *Christian* wife, a *Christian* attorney, a *Christian* manager, or a *Christian* minister. And that qualifier "Christian" tells you and me how it is that we are striving to live our vocations.

Christian faith is not just a set of beliefs. Christian faith is a way of seeing. It is a vision of others, our world, and ourselves. Faith in Jesus Christ gives us a way to make sense of who we are and what we should do, of what we value and what our priorities in life should be. It makes sense of why we choose to live one way and refuse to live another way. It explains why we go to church, why we celebrate the Eucharist, and why we want to pass on this precious faith to others.

The problem for many of us (indeed, for all of us, some of the time) is that our identity as Christians is not so firm. We understand ourselves in many ways. There are many elements of our identity, and being Christian is all too often just one part of our identity along with so many other components. Sadly, our sense of self and our vision of the world is sometimes more formed by what we pick up from our society—from our upbringing, from the media, from our wider society—than from the Gospel and from the faith of the Church. In the end, if we were to make a list of what makes us who and what we are, where our values come from, and how we set our life's priorities, where would "Christian faith" appear on this list?

Christian faith gives us a way of viewing ourselves in relation to others and to the world. We can speak of the "eyes of faith," a Christian "vision," or a Christian "lens" for viewing the world. Christian faith is meant to enable and require us to see the world and other people and what is important in life in a particular way. The Christian vision, for example, reveals that the poor are blessed by God, that we should love our enemies, that we should forgive those who have harmed us, that we should reach out to the stranger, that suffering can be redemptive, that dying is a gateway to real life... and so many other realities that a worldly vision views as naïve or simply as silliness. Be that as it may, to be a Christian means that who we are, how we act, and how we relate to the people around us are formed and guided by this Christian vision and no other.

The problem is that we want to be able to wear glasses with two different lenses not adapted to one another. We understand ourselves to be followers of Jesus, and we believe that he tells us and shows us the truth about human living. But at the same time, we want to go on viewing life as getting ahead, having more, being liked and valued, having our way, and the rest. But we can't really see if we have two different lenses that aren't adapted to one another. Maybe we'd like to be able to wear one set of glasses sometimes and the other set at another time. But one of the lenses reveals the truth of reality and the other simply does not, at least not fully or reliably. And, sadly, there are Christians who really have just one set of glasses—their "worldly" glasses—who assess the Church and their participation in it according to the reality that "the world" reveals to them.

Christian conversion involves seeing the world anew. As we sing in the Christian hymn *Amazing Grace*: "I was blind but now I see." In faith, we see ourselves anew: We are reborn. When God leads us into a real adult acceptance of our faith—the decision to be Christian—it is like putting on new glasses that enable us finally to see the world as it really is. We realize that how we saw before—to the degree that we could really see at all—was incomplete, blurred, or simply wrong. To the Christian, so much of the worldly vision is either false or blindness—just as Christian truth appears unreal to the vision of the world.

The explicit experience of this newness of vision is perhaps most evident in the conscious experience of an adult conversion—what happens at a special moment or in response to some special event. Some Christians have had such experiences in which their lives, their sense of what truly matters in life, and their priorities were simply turned upside down. Suddenly, they saw anew. Perhaps we can think of the story of the conversion of Saint Paul (Acts 9:1–19). As a faithful and fervent Pharisee and active persecutor of the Church, he saw reality in one way. But then he encountered Jesus along the way, and he was struck physically blind. (In fact, the Christian reader knows that Paul had really been suffering all along from a deeper blindness of which he wasn't even aware.) Then, visited by God's messenger, "something like scales fell from his eyes, and his sight was restored"(Acts 9:18).He saw anew.

Some Christians have special experiences akin to that of Saint Paul, but this new Christian vision of ourselves in relation to the world can also unfold more gradually. In fact, it must always grow clearer, stronger, and more inclusive of the entirety of life. For many of us, it is really a process by which a Christian comes to a mature acceptance of his or her commitment to faith over time; but this acceptance is also a decision.

Christians Are Called to Become Saints

We must decide to be Christian. We must each take up, by choice, the invitation of Jesus to become his disciple, and we must accept his invitation to become nothing less than saints. We must decide that, to the degree that it is in our power, cooperating with God's grace, we will become saints...and nothing less. My former abbot, Lambert Reilly, OSB, likes to say that, on Judgment Day, sanctity is the only success that God will acknowledge. It's the only "success" worth achieving.

The Second Vatican Council taught us that we are called, by virtue of our baptism, to be holy. We are called to be saints—all of us, and not just a special handful of Christians. Sinners are called by God to enter into friendship with him, into a deep communion with him. God calls us to draw close to him, to become like him, to share his very divine life. And this is true whatever our particular state in life.

In a sense, we are already saints. In his letters, Saint Paul frequently addresses his fellow Christians as "the saints" (Ephesians 1:1; Philippians 1:1). We are made holy by our union with Christ in baptism and our communion with him in the Eucharist. At the same time (and perhaps this is more true to our personal experience), we are always sinners on the road to holiness, the great goal of our lives. We are saints who are invited and challenged to become ever more truly saints.

Early Christian writers noted the distinction between being created in God's "image" and in God's "likeness" (Genesis 1:26). We are all created in the image and likeness of God as human beings. To be human is irrevocably to carry the divine *image*. But our *likeness* to God—that is, our resemblance to God—is destroyed or at least marred by the fact of sin. The Christian life, then, is the ongoing journey of conversion in which those created in the image of God strive, with God's help, to restore their likeness to God. Or to put it another way, we must strive to restore our likeness to an all-holy God.

The call to holiness is both an awesome and wondrous invitation to sinners, as well as a great, lifelong challenge. And, if we are to become what we were meant to be, it is an invitation and a challenge that we simply cannot refuse. If it is true that the Almighty and transcendent God calls mere creatures—sinners—into the deepest communion with him in this life and in the life to come, then how could it be possible to refuse? Can it be that God holds out the invitation of union with him—again, in heaven and *in this life*—and that it would really be possible for us to respond: "Well, I'll take it in the life to come, but I'd rather not have it in this life?" Could there be a more ungrateful response?

Each and every Christian is called to holiness...and nothing less. The sad fact is that too few Christians really realize it. Maybe many of us unconsciously would really rather not recognize this vocation to sanctity because we don't really want to embrace the challenge that it entails. Or perhaps, realistically, Christians have very little opportunity to be awakened to this great truth and good news. I suspect that few priests, religious educators, and Christian parents realize or fully embrace this vocation to holiness for themselves. How, then, can they hold out the invitation and challenge to those with whom they are sharing the faith? How can Christians accept an invitation that they really have never received? As Saint Paul says about the acceptance of the faith more broadly: "But how are they to call on one in whom they have not believed? And are they to believe in one of whom they have never heard? And how are they to hear without someone to proclaim him" (Romans 10:14)? How can Christians learn of their exalted calling if their pastoral leaders and teachers do not tell them...and *show* them?

To say that we are called to holiness is really to say again that there can be no halfheartedness or lukewarm behavior in the Christian life. We must decide that we will respond, with God's help, to Christ's invitation to be his followers; and we must decide to respond wholeheartedly to God's call to be nothing less than saints. Each Christian must say a firm and daily "no!" to mediocrity, halfheartedness, and minimalism.

In reality, in the decision to be a Christian and to become a saint, we set out on a difficult, daily journey. It is not easy to be a

Christian, much less a saint. Surely this has always been the case. In many ways, our contemporary society, with all of its options and contrary voices, makes it even harder. One of my colleagues likes to say: "It's not hard to be a Christian...the hard part is doing it one day after another." And so it is. In the chapters that follow we will see more of what this journey entails and how we are helped along the way by God and by our fellow Christians in the body of Christ.

Questions for Reflection

* *Taking seriously the challenge of Jesus to follow him without reserve, do you feel that you have held back? If so, how and why?*

* *Can you identify in your own life the ways that the qualifier "Christian" makes a difference in your work, your relationships, and your life in general (that is, as a Christian husband, a Christian physician, a Christian parent, a Christian wife, a Christian police officer, etc.)?*

* *In examining your own life, what are some of the major factors, influences, and experiences (whether positive or negative) that have made you the person you are today? Where does "Christian faith" fit into that list? How does its influence manifest in your life?*

* *What might holiness look like in your life?*

* *What would have to change or develop in your life in order for you to become a saint?*

* *Are there signs in your own life of mediocrity or halfheartedness in living as a Christian?*

Prayer

Gracious God of life and light, you have given to me the precious gift of Christian faith, a way of seeing myself and the world, a way of seeing the truth. Forgive my willing blindness and open my eyes more completely so that I may see you, myself, and the world around me with the sure vision of Jesus. Give me true sight so that I can walk in the path of the holiness to which you have so wonderfully called me. I ask this in the name of Jesus Christ, my Lord. Amen.

CHAPTER

THE WORLD IN WHICH
WE FIND OURSELVES

As a pastor, I am deeply inspired by the many men and women who are so obviously dedicated to their Catholic faith. Some come to weekday Mass regularly, a few of them coming as much as an hour early in order to pray quietly in the church before Mass. The confessions of such Catholics are sincere and demonstrate their deep concern over even minor sins and omissions. They participate actively in the life of the parish and contribute to it, as they are able, in many different ways. They are regulars at adult faith formation offerings, Bible studies, and parish missions. They struggle to live faithfully in the midst of the various demands on their lives—as spouses, parents, grandparents, catechists, church volunteers, workers, etc.—all the while trying to find time for prayer, some spiritual reading, participation in the sacraments, and service to others.

There is such a spiritual hunger in our world and in our Church today, and these faithful Catholics have recognized their hunger. They actively seek out what will feed their longing and their need. They deserve to be fed. Surely, God wants them to be fed.

Sadly, at the same time, there are many other Catholics (and probably most of us, at least some of the time) who do not even realize the depth of their hunger. They are so full of the things that this world has to offer, so busy reaching out for what will not ultimately satisfy or nourish them that they have no inkling of what they most truly and deeply need.

Studies tell us that regular Mass attendance is down in parishes across the country. And while there are so many dedicated Catholics who would not miss Mass except for the gravest of reasons, there are at least as many who come "most of the time" or "as long as nothing really important comes along" or from time to time. In fact, there appear to be a lot of Catholics who are proud of the fact that they come to Mass "most of the time." "Who, after all," a parishioner recently challenged me, "goes to Mass all the time?" (Well, in fact, quite a few Catholics do just that.)

The Church is losing people. I don't mean to other denominations, though that is a reality as well. I mean losing people to no faith, to nothing, to pure unreflective secularity. Many of these Catholics are not so much deciding to leave as much as they are just drifting away, losing interest, distracted by other realities in their lives. In their own minds, they have not stopped being Catholics. They are just Catholics without regular church involvement, without any regular spiritual practice or discipline—without much thought about God or faith or church. Being Christian or being Catholic is no longer a fundamental or even a necessarily essential element of their personal identity, world view, or set of values. In some real sense, of course, they are still Catholics, but it is not clear—least of all to them—how this is so or what it means.

In my own parish, I see parents faithfully dropping their kids off for weekly religious education—parents and kids whom I will not see in church the next Sunday. I hear confessions regularly in the parish religious education program, and I hear too many children confess that they don't go to Mass on Sundays. When I ask why, they tell me their parents don't bring them. I see kids and their parents in preparation for first confession, first Communion, and confirmation whom I rarely, if ever, see in church. (What does it mean to ensure that your children are prepared for first confession or Communion if you never intend to bring them to church again?)

Apparently, a lot of Catholic parents continue to have a sense that the religious education of their children is important. They are maintaining, at some level, their family's religious tradition (much to the relief of more traditional grandparents). But many of these parents don't seem to think their own active participation in the life of the church and in the religious formation of their children needs to be a priority in their lives. But without follow-up in the home, in cooperation with parish religious education, without active sacramental practice as a family, without parental involvement and commitment to be even a part of their children's faith formation (beyond dropping them off, once a week, for an hour), how can this drifting out of the Catholic Church be slowed and stopped?

In preparing parents for the baptism of their infants, I often encounter couples who are interested in their faith and practice it faithfully. They accept with apparent seriousness the commitments that they will make in presenting their infant children for the sacrament of baptism, the task of being the "first and best" of teachers of their children in the faith. At the same time, I regularly encounter parents who, it seems to me, have come to baptismal preparation just because they have to; they nod their heads, acknowledging the words that they will say in the rite...and then, sadly, after the baptism, I will see them no more often than I had seen them in the months and years that preceded it. How will these newly baptized children ever really be formed in the faith in a way that will allow them to take up that faith with consistent and firm belief?

Of course, God is a God of surprises, always inviting all of us into a real and deeper life of faith. God is always pouring out a superabundance of grace. God never gives up. We are always in God's hands. It is certainly not my place to judge any individual or couple or to police their religious observance.

There are undoubtedly many reasons for this drifting away from the practice of the faith. In any case, my ultimate purpose here is not to focus on the reasons for this drift but rather on its consequences. At the same time, it can be said that some reasons are well-known or seemingly obvious. Research tells us that each recent generation of Catholics has less sense of institutional belonging and less understanding of the basics of their faith. The turmoil and changes of the Second Vatican Council in the mid-1960s brought great renewal but also widespread confusion about the basics of Catholic faith. Pre-Vatican II parents did not know what to teach their Vatican II children, who know even less what to pass on to their post-Vatican II children. And so each generation knows less and feels fewer adherences to the Church.

Even if basic Christian beliefs are well-known, they are often viewed, along with everything else, through the subjectivistic and relativistic lenses of our contemporary society. We unavoidably view the world from our own perspectives. But today there is a rampant doubt about or even denial of objective truth. Even recognizing that there is a lot of ambiguity in the world—that things aren't always black and white in a complex world—in our society, we doubt that anyone could state a truth, a value, or a moral principle that would be true for each and every person in our society. And so today we hear sincere people say things like, "Well, *I* wouldn't do that particular action. It would be wrong for *me*...and *maybe* for you, too. But who am I to say what *you* should do in your life? If you *really* believe that it's OK for you, and you're not hurting anyone...well...."

If it were a just matter of picking the right pair of pants or model of car, that kind of thinking would be just fine. But the same attitude is applied, even by sincere Christians, to the basic and urgent moral issues of our society, from abortion, to sexuality, to end-of-life issues. How can anyone adhere firmly to the Christian faith, to its fundamental beliefs and practices, with the attitude that it's all relative?

So many people today (Catholics included) decide on the degree of their church affiliation, participation, and attendance (if any) based on how they feel, on the other things that they personally feel to be important for them during that time in their lives, or on what is "moving" them at any particular period in their lives. This is the way it is in a world in which everything is judged by our subjective, felt experience of whatever reality we see before us.

As in every age, Christians feel the unavoidable pull of "worldly" pleasures and prizes. Christian faith has always competed with "worldly" values. But today, in an economically troubled but still largely affluent society, the allure of material things is so much stronger because in fact they are so much more available, attainable, and therefore so much more attractive. It is just easier to be materialistic when there are a lot more glitzy, high-tech, high-end material things that are available to be desired, coveted, pursued, attained, and then replaced with something still glitzier, more high-tech, etc.

Today there are so many Christians trying to straddle two worlds. (To a degree, that describes all of us.) They have been raised as Catholics and believe, in some basic, though indistinct way. Many view themselves as Catholics, though they don't much think about what that might mean or what this demands of them. They still come to Mass most of the time and feel they should—though, beyond custom and family expectations, they may not be sure why. They want to hold on to their Christianity, to their Catholicity. They feel they should pass it on to their children (or at least expose their children to it). But at the same time, they want to live like everyone else: to get ahead, to have what people have, to find happiness.

Whatever the reasons, or however accurate any particular part of my brief analysis might be, Catholics are drifting away from the practice of their faith. Being Christian is no longer a central element of their personal identity. Christian values no longer guide their lives—except to the degree that these values remain in some form in our wider society. They are still "nice" people, perhaps upstanding and model citizens, good neighbors, reliable friends; but the fact that they remain Christian has little impact on how they live their lives, why they are the people they are, or why they do the things they do.

I see the sad reality of this Catholic "drift" especially in moments of tragedy and trial. I visit the hospital room of a person who, on admittance, indicated that she is a member of my parish. When I walk in, I discover a person I have never met and have, to my knowledge, never seen. I go to the funeral home to meet the family of a person recently deceased. He had once been a member of the parish. He was baptized a Catholic. Maybe the parish secretary remembers that the family used to go to church "years ago." But neither the deceased nor his spouse nor the adult children have darkened the door of the parish church in decades.

These are undoubtedly moments when evangelization can happen, when a renewed invitation can be offered, and when faith can be reawakened. And there is no doubt that these tragic times are often situations in which little can really be said at the moment to relieve the sense of loss and sadness. It's not a time for glib or easy statements of piety—and much less a time for a check on regular Mass attendance. It's a time to be present, to listen, to pray.

At the same time, what do I as a minister of the Church have to offer a patient or a family who has only the remnants of Christian faith and identity? What is the common language we speak? Yes, we have a language shared by all men and women by virtue of our humanity: anxiety, pain, loss, suffering; the language of silent, human presence and companionship. Of course! And those are no small things to offer. But what of the riches of the Christian faith? What of hope? What of the truth of the message of the cross? What of trust and surrender? What of a God who brings unexpected good out of suffering and loss? What of new life, life beyond, unimagined life in abundance?

Though I am focusing on the negative aspects of our contemporary world, I do not mean to suggest that the situation is without hope. In fact, it is ultimately quite to the contrary. My purpose is not to bash the world and our society. If Jesus came not to condemn the world but to save it, how could his followers do otherwise? I do not mean to suggest (at least not with too much personal conviction) that the world is "going to hell in a hand basket." So much could be said that is positive and right in our world. There is so much progress on so many fronts. But I do want to point to the reality in which every Christian finds himself or herself today. This is the world in which every Christian lives, comes to an identity as a person and as a Christian, and must set priorities and make decisions.

In sum, the Church is in trouble. Yes, our Lord promised that the gates of hell will never prevail against the Church. Yes, the Spirit is at work at every moment in the world and in our individual lives. Maybe it would be better to say, for my purposes here, that we are in trouble—those of us who want to live authentically as Christians in the world. Again, the Spirit is with us at every moment. It's just that the world, for better and for worse, is usually easier to see; its voice is easier to hear; its allurements more tangible.

We are in trouble. But the threat is not laws forbidding the practice of religion. It's not the danger of active persecution. The danger is "seepage"—that our faith, and we with it, will seep out of the Church along with so many others. The danger is that we will drift away as it seems that so many others have done or are doing.

Surely this is a problem that must be confronted at a number of different levels, in a variety of ways and methods. I have no doubt about the profound insight of Pope John Paul II about the need for a "new evangelization," calling people to the faith but also calling people *back* into the faith and active participation in the life of the Church, as well as our own daily renewed encounter with the Good News. As a priest and a pastor, and as a seminary educator, I see that the work of evangelization is the fundamental task of priests and, in their own way, of all of the Church's ministers. But my purpose here in this book, in the face of the current situation, is to suggest that for each of us, in our own lives, we must *decide* to be Christian. This has always been the case, of course, for every Christian in every age. But it's true even more so today. Today, in the face of the drift that we experience all around us, each of us must decide: "I will be a Christian. I will be a follower of Jesus Christ. My faith will be central to who and what I am. I will form my identity, set my priorities, make my decisions, and establish and live my relationships as a disciple of Jesus. I will be an active participant in the life of the Church, being supported and guided by it and contributing to its life for the sake of others."

What does this mean and how do I live it?

Questions for Reflection

* *Do you agree with the conclusion that many Catholics are drifting away from the faith? If so, to what do you attribute this drift? What can we as individuals and local communities of faith do about it?*

* *In what ways does the society in which we live support your life as a Christian? What values do you see in our world that affirm our values as Christians?*

* *In what ways does our society make authentic Christian living more difficult? What passes as values in our society that are not, from a Christian perspective, truly valuable?*

* *What might make a good Christian distinct from a nice person in our society who has no faith?*

Prayer

God of the universe, of all that is and is yet to be, you have brought me wondrously into existence in this time and place. You have blessed me with all the wonders and beauty of creation and with the precious people who have taught, formed, nourished, and challenged me in my life. Even as I praise you for all the good that surrounds me in this world, I pray for your help to draw me away from all that is false, all that is not worthy, all that is not in accord with your loving will for me and for this world. This I ask in the name of Jesus. Amen.

LOVE COMES FIRST

"In this is love, not that we loved God but that he loved us...."

Every Christian knows that love is at the heart of the life and teaching of Jesus. The two great commandments instruct us to love God and neighbor (Matthew 22:36–39; Mark 12:28–31; John 13:34–35. See also Matthew 5:43–48; Luke 6:27–35). In fact, the teaching of Jesus is all about love. Furthermore, his life is its perfect witness: reaching out to the outcasts, extending concern for the poor and the sick, demonstrating a humble service to others, and most perfectly surrendering himself selflessly to death on the cross in order to save sinners.

Love is at the heart of who Jesus is and what he taught, and so it is at the heart of Christian living. Every Christian knows this fundamental truth, however imperfectly we might live it or understand exactly what it should mean for our daily living. But the fact remains that we will profoundly misunderstand what love really is and how we must live it unless we see the truth of what Saint John the Evangelist says so firmly: "In this is love, not that we loved God but that he loved us..." (1 John 4:10). In fact, Jesus is the incarnate revelation of this most basic truth of God's prior and perfect love for us sinners.

God's love for sinners is at the heart of the Good News that Jesus came to bring. It is the fundamental truth that is grasped by a real Christian faith. God loves sinners. God loves *this* sinner. In faith, we come to see the wonder of the simple statement: "God so loved the world..." (John 3:16). And in faith, we can marvel with Saint Paul that Christ died for us while we were yet sinners, helpless, even enemies (Romans 5:6–10).

Our love for God and our love for God's children are grounded in this Good News. The command to love is therefore not some merely external command to be followed simply because God inexplicably requires it. Rather, it is the response to the discovery in faith of God's undeserved love for me and for all of sinful humanity as well as the recognition of the divine invitation to enter into communion. Love is also a command, as we shall see, only because sin makes us both blind to the truth of the Good News and to the shape of our authentic response and because sin makes us unable to live it faithfully.

When we know in faith that we are loved by the God of Jesus Christ, we find reason to love. We are empowered to love. Love becomes the only response that makes sense. If, in our daily lives, we sometimes find it difficult to love God as faithfully, as consistently, as wholeheartedly as we know that we ought...and likewise find it equally difficult, at times, to love our irritating, ungrateful, all-too-human neighbor in practice, then we must return to the source of our loving. We will find renewed reason and empowerment to love by recalling the divine love that calls us to love in return. What is the purpose of the traditional encouragement to meditate on the cross of Jesus (whether in the liturgy of Holy Week, the prayerful rereading of the Gospel passion narratives, the Sorrowful Mysteries of the Rosary, or the Way of the Cross) except to fuel within us a deeper conviction, appreciation, and wonder at the love of God shown to us in Christ Jesus, calling us to a humble, grateful, and loving response.

The truth is that we are made to love. We are most authentically what we are meant to be when we give ourselves generously in love to and for others. The fundamental truth of our existence as human beings is that we are created in the image of God. As Saint John the Evangelist tells us: God is love.

Love is not just an activity of God, nor is it just a personal characteristic of God. God *is* love. The doctrine of the Trinity reveals to us how this statement is true. For all eternity, the Father has given himself, poured out himself on the Son, and the Son has responded perfectly to the Father with his own self-giving love. This mutual self-giving, this love at the heart of God is the Holy Spirit. God is love; God is selfless self-giving; and we are created in this divine image. And so we are most truly who we are and what we were created to be in giving ourselves to and for others. Here we find our truest happiness and authentic fulfillment. And, on the contrary, we contradict our very nature, who and what we most truly are, in our selfishness and self-centeredness. We can all say with Saint Thérèse, the Little Flower, "My vocation is love," no matter what particular way of life we choose or are called to live.

The command of Jesus to love reminds us of our truest—and really our only—path to happiness and fulfillment. The command to love God and neighbor is in no way just some external command that we follow simply because we are required to do so. The twofold command is therefore really the offer of light in the darkness, a mirror for those who want to see themselves as they really are, a road map for those who are lost in a world of sin, a hand stretched out to those who are blind and unable to walk properly along the path. And in this, Jesus is himself the key. In his teaching, life, death, and resurrection, we discover the Good News of God's wondrous love for us, despite our refusals of the divine love; and so, in him, we find renewed reason to love. In Jesus, God's incarnate love, we learn what love truly is and how to love both God and neighbor. In the power of the death and resurrection of Jesus, we are enabled by the outpouring of the Holy Spirit to overcome the reality of sin and to love as we ought, as we are commanded, and as we are meant to do.

Love should be—and must become—our most fundamental stance, priority, and inclination in life. Our failure to love is not simply or even primarily disobedience but rather a contradiction of and harm to ourselves. Each time we fail to act generously and selflessly toward others, we diminish ourselves and make ourselves less authentically who we were meant to be and indeed less authentically human.

This is the reason that love is the fundamental command of Jesus.

Love is the starting point, the key that interprets every other law and commandment. When Jesus was asked to name the greatest command, he immediately named the love of God and neighbor; and he affirmed that all of the law and prophets are contained in these two commands (Matthew 22:40). Every other command is a specification of this great command and of the basic truth of our being. Without love, we fail to see the rest of the laws, norms, and rules in their proper place. This is the fundamental truth that Jesus was trying to teach the Pharisees in the controversies recorded in the Gospels.

In his 1993 encyclical *Veritatis Splendor,* paragraph 22, Pope John Paul II repeated the question of Saint Augustine: Does love bring about the keeping of the commandments or does the fulfillment of the commandments bring about love? And the pope responded with Saint Augustine that it is obvious that it is love that must come first, because without love, what reason does one have to follow the commandments?

Saint Augustine also famously said, "Love and do what you will." Obviously, the great saint and doctor of the Church was not inviting us to licentiousness, doing as we please as long we retain warm and pleasant feelings toward others. The fact is that if we truly were able to love, we would *want* to act rightly toward God and neighbor, and we would be empowered to do so. Love would ensure that we would never seek less than the good of our neighbor and never be content with mere minimums.

It is in this sense that we can understand the teaching of Saint Paul in his Letter to the Romans (13:8–10): "The one who loves another has fulfilled the law. The commandments, 'You shall not commit adultery; You shall not murder; You shall not steal; You shall not covet'; and any other commandment, are summed up in this word, 'Love your neighbour as yourself.' Love does no wrong to a neighbour; therefore, love is the fulfilling of the law."

When I teach moral theology in the seminary, I tell the seminarians that I believe the first task of a priest as a moral teacher is evangelization. Unless people recognize the Good News of God's unmerited and extravagant love for sinners, until their love for God is awakened by the recognition that God has first loved us, the commandments and all of the moral teachings of the Church—true and important in themselves—will seem merely like some extrinsic command, some divine whim imposed from outside, or the old-fashioned, out-of-touch dictums of ecclesiastical prudes. Love makes sense of the commandments; love gives us reason to seek out those rules that will help us to respond to the love given us; and love moves us to do more than what we are commanded.

It should be clear that the love of which we speak is not some superficial feeling. Love is not primarily a warm feeling toward others. Love is an act of the will; it is a commitment; it is a decision about a way of being in relationship with others and being in the world. Love is not a matter of liking other people. It is about placing others' needs ahead of my wants, giving ourselves generously to and for others, serving others as the teaching and example of Jesus make clear.

At the same time, love does not ask us to become doormats, to let others take advantage of us, nor are we to take advantage of others. The other-directedness of love does not require us to accept abuse nor to tolerate it. Often, in such situations, we do no one a favor by allowing someone to harm us. This harm will most likely contribute to the continued harm of others. We cannot forget that we are commanded to love our neighbor *as we love ourselves*. We, too, are created in God's image, worthy of respect and justice. But in a world of individualism and frequent selfishness, most of us need more encouragement to think of others than to think first of guarding our own legitimate rights.

Philosophically, love has been described as possessing two elements: benevolence (*willing* the good for others) and beneficence (*doing* the good for others). When sincere Christians seek to love those who have harmed them in some way, forgiveness sometimes requires time and healing. While we cannot remain content with harboring hard feelings toward others, we must begin with benevolence (*willing* the good for the other, which we may not yet *feel* like doing) and beneficence (*doing* the good, where possible) for the person whom we have not yet been able fully to forgive. If our feelings were fully in line with our will, we would in fact feel our love for our neighbor, as Jesus felt love for the leper, for the sinner, and toward those who betrayed him. But all in due time....

Ultimately, however, real Christian love is not content with willing the good and doing the good, although those are essential elements. Love always seeks the day when our self-giving love will be reciprocated, when love will be mutual, when our love truly mirrors the mutual self-giving within the heart of the Trinitarian God who is love. The love that Christians share within the Christian community, most especially the love of husband and wife, are meant to shine as an example of that perfect love even in this world.

Still, in this life, in this world of sin, love must often take the form of self-giving, as Jesus illustrated on the cross, inviting a loving response from the other. Confronted by the refusal, the denial, the betrayal, the abandonment, the ridicule, Jesus nonetheless gave himself for others on the cross. He gave himself even for those who consciously and actively refused his love, who harmed him and put him to death. He did so, of course, to invite and enable the response of love from those who brought about his death—those in first-century Palestine as well as in twenty-first century America. The love of Jesus, divine love, always seeks a return. And, thanks be to God, divine love never gives up.

The command of Jesus to love is a twofold command. It has two essential and inseparable parts: love of God and love of neighbor. As Saint John reminds us, we cannot say that we love God while failing to love our neighbor (1 John 4:20). If we love God in grateful and humble response to the divine love for us, then we will we want to love who God loves and as God loves. We will love God in God's children; we will love God in those who bear the divine image; we will love all those whom God loved so much that God sent his only Son to die for them. In loving the people standing before us, in action, whoever it might be, we love the God who is the parent, the Creator, the Savior, the ground of being of both us and them.

This is the message, told from another perspective, of the great judgment scene in the Gospel of Matthew (25:31–46). To love in action, the poor, the stranger, the hungry, the naked—with whom I have no personal relationship, who may well prove ungrateful or unworthy in practical terms, who may be superficially unattractive to me—this is the concrete sign of the authentic love of God. Again, as Saint John reminds us, those who say they love the God they cannot see, while failing to love the brother or sisters whom they can see, are liars.

The Christian life is and must be a life of love—love as an act of the will, a decision, a commitment, a way of living and relating. It must be lived out each day, in each situation, with each person, practically and not as a mere sentiment or noble but unrealized intention.

How, then, can we grow in such love? By daily reminding ourselves of the divine love, by meditating on the love God has shown throughout history but especially in the saving death and resurrection of Jesus, by pondering again and again the wondrous cross of our Savior, by recalling the countless blessings that God has showered on us and the unimaginable future that God has promised us. In short, as Pope John Paul II urged us, we must daily reevangelize ourselves, recalling each day the Good News of God's love for sinners...like me.

We grow in love by drawing close to God and by opening ourselves to the Spirit so that the divine love can fill us, move us, and slowly transform us. Without God's love at work in us in his Spirit, we cannot love as we ought. Most profoundly and deeply, it is our task and goal, more and more, to unite ourselves to God's love for our neighbor.

Then, love becomes everything. Following the commandments becomes love. Serving others, forgiving others, reaching out to others—all become love. Prayer becomes love; love expresses itself in prayer, whether our prayer is dry like the desert or as sweet as the song of angels. All becomes a grateful and humble self-giving to God in worship and for others.

Saint Thomas Aquinas defined love as "friendship with God." This is the great mutuality that true love seeks—that God has first and always sought. It is God's gift. God has given all, to and for sinful creatures, and has deeply invited us into divine friendship. In this life, we begin to live this friendship as an anticipation of sharing perfectly in the Trinitarian community by loving God and neighbor, conforming ourselves to God's will and God's ways, drawing close and surrendering ourselves in trust to him.

The Good News of God's love for us in Christ is the ground and the empowerment for us to decide to set out along the path of love that leads to eternal life with and in the triune God.

Questions for Reflection

* *Based on your reflection and experience, how would you personally define love?*

* *What stories in the Scriptures make God's love come alive for you?*

* *In addition to the witness of Jesus, who has been a particular witness of the meaning of love to you? How so?*

* *How has God's love for you been evident in your life? How have you experienced it?*

* *Where in your life do you find the greatest difficulty in loving God or neighbor?*

* *How can you try to love God more deeply and completely?*

Prayer

God of love, how amazing is your loving concern for all you have created! How unimaginable a love that can see through my sin and the sin of the world around me! How constant, how faithful, how sweet is your love for me and for all that you have created! Give me eyes to see that love more truly. Give me a heart more open to receive it. Give me a desire and a decision to respond, to share, and to rejoice! In Jesus Christ, you have perfectly manifested your infinite love. In his name I pray. Amen.

4

LOVE AND GRATITUDE, GRATITUDE AND LOVE

Recent research at the University of California-Davis reveals the real-life benefits of taking time to "take stock" of one's blessings in life.[1] It turns out that a habit and a spirit of gratitude is good for your health. People who take time daily to think about and even write down things for which they are grateful have a more positive outlook on life. They generally are more optimistic, are less likely to feel ill, are more likely to make progress toward their own personal goals, tend to be more empathetic toward others, have a greater likelihood to reach out to give a hand to others, and are inclined to be less concerned about material things. It pays to take time to be grateful in life. This same research tells us that, while a disposition of gratitude does not depend on religious faith, faith enhances the ability to be grateful.

In fact, it is easy to become focused on the negative, the problems of life. Often, there can be more than enough to draw our attention. Sadly, we all know people who seem unable to focus on anything but the negative, on what's wrong in their lives. Chronic illness, the daily burdens of declining health, loneliness, experiences of abandonment or betrayal, the daily care of the elderly and infirm family members—all of these and more can take their toll on our spirit, drawing our eyes away from the good that coexists with the bad. We can become trapped in our own negativity. Encountering such people, we can sympathize with the trials they face, even as we feel the weight of trying to engage them and open their eyes to the good.

I regularly encourage people to make a daily examen of blessings. In addition to taking stock of our failures and sin at the end of the day, we ought as well to take stock of the good that we have experienced that day—good that, as people of faith, we know comes from God's loving and bountiful hand. In faith, we can say that these good things are truly "blessings" from God. Without too much reflection, almost all of us can bring to mind so much for which we

---

1 http://psychology.ucdavis.edu/labs/emmons

ought to be grateful each day: life, health, a good meal, a good laugh, an unexpected encounter with a friend, a sunny day, flowers in the garden, a good read, a success at work, an insight into a problem. In fact, combined with a traditional examen of conscience, the recalling of life's blessings, a daily recall of gratitude, allows us to see our sin in sharper relief and thus moves us to a deeper conversion.

A habit of thanksgiving, consciousness of life's blessings, refusal to give into a spirit of negativity no matter the difficulty we face—all of these yield benefits to our health, prepare us to face life's problems with a more positive attitude, and just make us more pleasant people to be around.

Gratitude for What God Has Done

As people of Christian faith, we ought to foster a spirit of gratitude in ourselves for a more fundamental reason: because God, who is the source of all good things, deserves it. Research tells us of the benefits of gratitude, but gratitude to whom? Virtually anyone in our society would agree that we ought to "count our blessings." But by whom are we being "blessed?"

Christian faith reveals to us that every good thing comes from God's loving hand. Our reasons to be grateful are as fundamental as they are expansive. We exist for no other reason than because of God's love. Sinner or saint, God holds us in existence at every moment. All abilities, talents, and personal gifts we possess come from God. Each person in our lives is a unique and sacred divine gift to us and to the world, to be respected and cherished. We ourselves are also just such a gift—to ourselves—as well as a wonderful mystery to be discovered and developed.

Although we are sinners who have failed God time and time again—refused, betrayed, ignored, taken for granted—God always stands ready to forgive and help. And more, in God's incredible love, the Father sent his only Son to die for us sinners. As Saint Paul reminds us in his Letter to the Romans (5:8): "But God proves his love for us in that while we still were sinners Christ died for us."

In the end, we are not capable of the slightest good without God's help. Without grace, we cannot recognize the good to be done; we cannot rise to the challenge of choosing the good; we cannot embrace the good in action. God is truly and absolutely the source of all good—of all created good and of all moral good.

And so, we must be people with grateful spirits, not for any benefit to us, but rather because God simply deserves it. God deserves to be worshiped and adored simply because God is God; and God deserves to be thanked, even with the little that our thanksgiving can offer, because of all that God has done for us out of divine love and mercy. In this vein, the fourth common Mass preface addresses God: "For, although you have no need of our praise, yet our thanksgiving is itself your gift, since our praises add nothing to your greatness but profit us for our salvation."

Gratitude as Empowerment

Gratitude is a powerful incentive to live the Christian life in all seriousness and totality. The Christian life—good moral living and prayer—is, after all, fundamentally thanksgiving for Good News. The Good News is this: the all-holy God loves sinners and invites them into communion with the blessed Trinity and one another. Or, as we noted in the previous chapter, we love because we have come to see that God has first loved us. When our eyes have been opened in faith to this Good News, we want to respond in prayer and in a life that honors God and shapes us into the divine image as we accept the invitation to enter into communion with God and others.

The daily demands of Christian living, in a broad sense, as well as the Church's moral teaching on major moral questions, is really fairly clear to most of us who possess even a basic religious education. Is there really a Catholic who doesn't know what the Church teaches about abortion or sex outside of marriage? Would any of us be surprised to discover that we shouldn't gossip about others, that we should be generous to others, that we shouldn't encourage fantasies about others that fail to respect them but rather reduce them to attractive body parts? The problem of daily Christian living is not generally conceptual clarity. Yes, sometimes, situations are complex, and prudent reflection and careful discernment are necessary; but the problem for us, usually, is really motivation and empowerment to see clearly and especially to act rightly.

As noted earlier, without a recognition and a sense of gratitude at the wonder of the Good News and of God's love for us, we feel little reason to attend to rules that, from the perspective of our society, seem merely old-fashioned, externally imposed, and out of step with the "real world." But when our eyes are opened to what God has done, is doing, and has promised to do for us, we feel abundant reason to strive to live as God wills and commands, knowing that what the God of Jesus Christ wills and commands is always what is best for us. We are then ready and even anxious to embrace what may seem to others to be "old-fashioned" or out of step with the way that other people live if only those rules will allow us to respond gratefully and humbly to God.

People who have had an adult conversion experience or at least have experienced the sense of spiritual awakening and renewal that can come, for example, from a particularly powerful retreat experience, know what I am describing here. An encounter with God's love for us fills us with zeal for real, serious, daily Christian living. The problem comes, of course, in sustaining this commitment (because the intensity of feeling never lasts). Perhaps many of us cannot recall particularly powerful experiences of God's love. Nonetheless, it is precisely by recalling the blessings, both great and small, that God has bestowed on us in his love that will empower us to respond faithfully to what God has done and promised.

The Catholic moral tradition provides abundant ways of understanding how the Church comes to arrive at sound moral rules and why this or that action is morally wrong. But the daily empowerment for moral living as Christians comes less from intellectual clarity and assent, and more from the love and thanksgiving that is both grounded in and feeds faith.

When we realize that we have received an awesome and undeserved gift, we are inspired to respond. The extravagance of God's love invites a generous response from the people of God, God's beloved. And there is no more awesome and undeserved gift than the love of God shown to us most especially in Jesus Christ. How can we glimpse even for a moment such divine extravagance and respond tepidly, halfheartedly? It is true that our response to God can never approach the wonder of what God gives and offers, but I think of the little hand-painted pictures that children give so proudly to their parents and grandparents—and that those parents and grandparents receive with such joy. Just so, God welcomes the humble offer of gratitude made by his children. Is it any wonder at all that we are taught that the Eucharist is the source and summit of the Christian life? This statement is profoundly true at many different levels, but here we merely recall that the word "Eucharist" means "thanksgiving." Our coming together at Mass to give thanks for all that God has done for us, individually and as a people, most especially in Jesus, is the source and empowerment of all Christian living. This communal act of thanksgiving in which we experience and anticipate the communion to which God's love invites sinners is the summit of our Christian living. In the Eucharist, we give ourselves to God in grateful response for all that God has done for us.

Love and gratitude. God's love for us comes first. Once our eyes and hearts are open to this great, undeserved gift, it is love born of gratitude that becomes our natural and fitting response. Our decision to follow Christ each day is born and nourished daily by humble gratitude for so wondrous a love. In order to live daily that love of God and neighbor, which is our thankful response, we must foster a spirit of gratitude: daily counting our blessings, meditating on the love of God made present throughout history but most especially in Jesus Christ, celebrating and renewing our gratitude in the Eucharist together with our brothers and sisters in faith.

Love yields gratitude; and gratitude empowers our loving.

Questions for Reflection

* *What motivates you to live the Christian life? Has gratitude played a role in your personal commitment?*

* *For what blessings are you especially grateful at this moment in your life?*

* *How do you experience the Eucharist as a celebration of thanksgiving, as its name suggests?*

* *How has gratitude motivated you to action in response to what another person has done for you?*

Prayer

God of all that is good and source of all blessings, how awesome is your love! How infinite your gifts and tokens of love for me and for the whole human family! If I could truly see just a fraction of those blessings, the fruit of your tender love, surely my heart would burst with joy and gratitude! Forgive now my blindness, my lack of gratitude, how closed my heart has been. Open my eyes! Open my heart! Let my entire being sing your praises, and let my life be a song of thanksgiving to you! In Jesus Christ I pray, through whom all good things flow. Amen.

5

THE TRAGIC REALITY OF SIN

If sin is the enemy of authentically and fully living our Christian commitment, then we are in serious trouble, because it appears that a lot of us Christians have little idea of the nature of the enemy we face.

It's commonplace these days for us middle-aged and older Catholics to note how few people seem to go to confession. Gone are the long lines to enter the confessionals on most Saturday afternoons. Undoubtedly there are a number of factors involved in this decline in sacramental practice, but it does not seem a significant stretch to think that confusion about sin is one of these factors. As a moral theologian, I am frequently asked to speak about a contemporary understanding of sin, because sincere, older Catholics are no longer sure what sin is, while younger Catholics are not sure that they ever really learned the meaning of sin. (All the while, of course, our society is telling us that there really isn't such a thing as sin—just mistakes and bad judgments.) As a pastor, it is not unusual for even older Catholics to tell me that one of the reasons they don't go to confession much anymore is that they are no longer sure what to confess. If it is true that we have moved away from an overemphasis on guilt and sin, a scrupulosity about confessing every questionable passing thought, it is no less true to say that we seem to have thrown out "the baby with the bath water."

Confusion after the Second Vatican Council, problems in religious education in recent decades, Catholic parents drifting away from their own commitments and thus neglecting the religious education of their children—whatever the factors that have weakened our sense of sin, we also face strong influences in our society that undermine an authentic understanding of sin and therefore our decision to be Christian. We live in a world of subjectivism in which people often don't believe in objective truth, in right and wrong independent of their own personal feelings and individual beliefs. What can sin really mean? What is its measure? Not objective standards and particular actions, not really even moral intentions in a classic sense; but rather, subjective feelings and felt motives. Sin in a world of subjectivism (even for those who sincerely wish to be Christian) would require them to have conscious and identifiable feelings of malice and ill will, the desire to hurt others, which many of us "good people" probably rarely have. How then can sex outside of marriage be a sin when "we love each other" or at least "we both consent and don't intend to hurt or use each other?"

Far *fewer* people are standing in confession lines, and far *more* people are standing in Communion lines. It seems today as if all Catholics automatically go to Communion, whether they have been to Mass recently or not, are living with someone outside of marriage, or have cheated their business or their workers of something that is fundamentally theirs. In the "old days," Catholics didn't go to Communion if they had failed to maintain the required eucharistic fast or failed to go to confession the day before (even if they were not aware of any mortal sin). So, at Communion time, many would not receive. Of course, it is a good thing that we have largely overcome scrupulosity about sin. Frequent Communion is to be encouraged as central to our active participation in the Eucharist. But somehow, without judging anyone in particular, we might imagine that at least a few of those people in line to receive Communion are guilty of sin sufficiently serious to warrant not going to Communion. My concern here, of course, is not the conditions under which one should or should not receive Communion, but rather the way in which current practice about confession and Communion suggests that there is a lack of understanding of sin and appreciation of what it might mean.

We are in a crisis about sin, and it exists at a fundamental level. What is sin? Do I personally sin? The most important issue here is not confessional practice or doctrinal clarity, each of which has its place. The crisis is far more foundational and critical to the faith itself. In essence, it is this: *No sin, no savior.* If we are not sinners— if I am not personally a sinner—then we don't need a savior. The consequences of this statement for the faith and for our reasons to adhere to it are mind-boggling. If I don't know that Jesus is my Savior, if I am not so sure from what I need to be saved, then what reason do I really have to adhere to him, to follow him, to trust in him? Most Christians, I imagine, would never want to say they don't need a savior—that Jesus didn't have to die for them personally—but without an understanding of sin and their need, it is no wonder that many Christians are, at best, halfhearted in following him. For too many Christians, Jesus seems to be some hazy figure that we know we must not abandon completely and whom we have some vague reason to follow. We're just not sure why, and we don't really see the need for the totality of his claim on us.

Even if, at some level, we are ready to own up to our sin, to admit that we do need a savior, another issue follows: If we don't really know what sin is, then we have no idea how to develop and live a game plan to confront it. We are facing an enemy, but we don't know exactly what it is, how it works, and what our response should be.

If, in a previous time, Catholics placed too much emphasis on and lived in fear of a rigorous and exacting God who kept minute records of every fault in order to exercise his inexorable and just judgment, today we live with the image of a doting, forgetful Father who takes no note of our failures, who cares little about what we do or don't do, just as long as we don't set out to hurt someone else.

God is love, we assure ourselves. God is merciful. God is not vengeful. All of those statements are true. And because they are true, this loving and merciful God offers us the most intimate, eternal communion as a pure gift. God invites us, draws us, gives us grace to help us, forgives us, and helps us to start again when we fail. Our eternal destiny, and even our most authentic fulfillment and peace in this life, depends on our response to this divine invitation. The problem, the obstacle that gets in the way of our acceptance of that invitation, is not God. It's us. It's sin.

In the same way, the consequences of our sin are not so much in what God does. God is indeed a God of love and mercy, always and for everyone. The consequences are in what we do to ourselves, what we make ourselves to be, what we refuse to become.

"No" to God and the Selfishness of Sin

At its heart, to sin is to say "no" to God, to say "no" to the divine offer of love and communion, to refuse to become what God has made us to be. Sin is to refuse to trust in God, to surrender, to give ourselves to God as God has given himself to us most especially in his Son, Jesus Christ.

The meaning of sin becomes apparent in the account of the Fall in the Book of Genesis (3:1–24). Adam and Eve lived in paradise. They walked with God in the Garden in the cool of day. They lived in communion with God, enjoying all that God had so graciously given them. The whole world had been given to them, and they lived in harmony with it all.

What the serpent came to offer them was independence, autonomy, a life in which they could be the ones calling the shots. If they ate the forbidden fruit, they would become like gods. Yes, it was an act of disobedience, and sin thereafter will always have that aspect. But Adam and Eve were refusing dependence on God, a life in communion with God, a life in which they could live surrendered to God and live humbly from God's provident hand.

At one level, Adam and Eve got what the serpent had promised them. They became the masters of their own lives. But at a deeper level, the serpent had lied to them, because really there is no life apart from God, outside the divine will, that does not depend on God and on surrendering to him. There is no real life except in conformity with God's will and in communion with God.

Immediately upon eating the fruit, Adam and Eve realized they were naked, and they covered themselves. Until sin entered the story, Adam and Eve were naked, open and vulnerable to one another. As the story tells us, the coming of sin brings not only mutual blaming but the inability to become completely vulnerable without fear of exploitation or ridicule, even to the people we love and who love us. Adam and Eve covered themselves from one another, and they covered and tried to hide themselves from the God who had created them and walked with them in the Garden. What a change in the harmony and openness described only a few verses earlier! The story tells us that God punished Adam and Eve, driving them out of the Garden. But this "punishment" is nothing more than the consequence of their sin. They had said "no" to a life of simple trust in and communion with God. They had decided they wanted to be the masters of their own lives. And so the Garden was no longer a place for them. Alienated from God, from their proper relation with God, they were alienated from each other and from the created world with which they previously lived in such harmony. No longer was there complete security in another person nor in the created order. And so the children of Adam and Eve foolishly and futilely seek security, not in God from whom alone it can truly come, but in things of their own making, things they can possess, control, or hold.

The first book of the Bible describes for us the beginning and the reality of sin. And in the chapters that immediately follow, we see the first fratricide, division, boasting, and pride. Until the coming of Jesus, humankind's story is a history of God's continual offer of communion and the divine invitation to become what we were intended to be. Sadly, it's also a history of the human refusal and continued misguided and tragic effort to live autonomously from God, without trust and without surrender.

This is the sad reality of sin—all sin, every sin. The truth is that we would find our true peace, happiness, and fulfillment in surrender to and communion with God. But we are born with the consequences of that original sin, this deep-seated sense of being incomplete, lost, out of touch—which, apart from God, we are. But instead of turning to God and walking in trust as Adam and Eve had first done in the Garden, we set out to make ourselves the source of our own security. This useless search takes its own particular form in each of our lives, at different times. More and shinier possessions, more superficial respect from others, more control over others, more pleasures that we can manipulate, more power, more status, the ability to threaten others or establish dominance over them—these are just some of the forms that sin can take.

But whether it is greed, hurtful gossip, stealing, insults, lies, or the like, they are all forms of that foolish and futile effort to find security in ourselves rather than surrender to God and enter into divine communion. We are born with this tendency. We see it lived all around us from the moment that our own decision-making capacity begins to be formed. We have our own history of it and our own personally developed illusion that some day it will work for us. But it won't. It can't. It never will.

This is the history and the reality of sinful human existence... until the coming of Jesus. In Jesus, the Son of God took on human flesh. And, sharing our humanity, he did what no human person had done since Adam and Eve committed that first sin. Jesus said "yes" to the Father. He trusted, he surrendered, he abandoned himself to the Father's will. And he did so on the cross—betrayed, ridiculed, abandoned, defeated, suffering, dying—all of those things that would make us reach out for whatever security we could command for ourselves: angry words to lash out at others, resentment toward those who abandoned or betrayed us, even calling down angels to have our way. But Jesus just trusted, he surrendered, he abandoned himself. And so he reversed the response of Adam and Eve. He opened the gates of heaven, showed us the way to communion with God and made it possible to do the same, united with him.

Sin, False Self, True Self

We can rightly see sin as an action. In a particular situation, we say
"no" to God. We say "no" to the divine invitation, in the form of a
particular command, to be conformed and to commune with God.
And since the divine commands are always for our own good, not
just some arbitrary expression of a divine whim, we thereby also
frustrate our ability to become what we are meant to be.

Sometimes sin takes the form of a refusal to trust. In the face
of life's difficulties, trust can be a difficult thing. There is no sin
in experiencing the struggle. In the Garden of Gethsemane, Jesus
struggled, too, with the cross as it lay before him. But sometimes,
when we examine our lives, we see how little effort we have made
to trust in God—how we have lived according to our own efforts
to take care of things ourselves. In our failure to overcome the difficulty on our own, we see that we have made ourselves to be the
root of our own unhappiness, bitterness, and frustration. On the
other hand, often it is in our inevitable failure that we are open to
the grace to see that "what is needed is trust" (Mark 5:36).

When we look at our sinful actions—the particular things that
we have done contrary to God's will or the particular times that we
have refused to trust—we see deeper attitudes and habits. Even if
we have not done terrible things, we see in ourselves how we have
failed to respond to the divine invitation. We have not really tried
to draw close to God. We have lived life very much according to our
own choosing, in our own way. At times, this is as clear as a failure
to participate in the sacramental life of the Church or a failure to
try to pray or to grow in prayer. We see that we have really lived
according to the values and priorities of this world, rather than the
ways of God made evident in the life and teaching of Jesus.

When we look deeper still, we can see that sin has led us to
construct our lives into an edifice based on a flawed concept and
plan. Our true, authentic existence can be found only in com-

munion with God. We are created in the divine image, made to live with God forever. Indeed, God holds us in existence at every moment. Sinner or saint, we would not exist unless God held us in existence. But the path to our fulfillment and destiny is in consciously and freely conforming ourselves to God and drawing close to God in prayer and in love. This is the path of growing in the freedom precisely to be able to surrender and give ourselves to God more completely.

Because of our fundamental temptation not to surrender to God in trust, because of the example that we see all around us and follow in our choices, we construct for ourselves a kind of "false self." We think we are autonomous, that we can and do "make it" on our own. We are blind to what is truly valuable, to what we ought to pursue in this life. We buy into the false values of this world: getting ahead, appearances, consumerism, materialism, individualism. But this is a false self. It is a sinful self in that it is built on the blindness caused by sin. Yet we live in and from it every day. We think that this is the real world, while the world of faith, of following Jesus and his teaching without compromise, is some idealistic or even unrealistic expectation.

Conversion

We desperately need to be free. We need to overcome our blindness so we can see what truly matters in life, what is worth pursuing, what we ought to be, and the path that we must follow. We need to have our eyes opened so we can see reality as it is and ourselves as we are. We need for the false, constructed self—the phony and sinful self—to die with Christ on the cross so we can truly live. We need to become free so we can choose life with Christ, a life in communion with and surrendered to God. In short, we need conversion—ongoing, deeper, daily conversion.

"I am the greatest sinner of all." This seems the almost commonplace claim of many of the saints. On the surface, the statement seems ridiculous, at best a pious exaggeration of reality. Compared to us, the saints are not sinners at all. And yet the saints mean what they say. The closer they draw to God, the more they see their sin. It is like drawing an object into the light. At a distance, in dim lighting, an object can look perfect, flawless. But as it is drawn into the light, its flaws, its defects, its imperfections become apparent. And so it is with the saints. They are not judging themselves against the values of the world. It is true that many saints were not murderers, thieves, or adulterers. But because they see more clearly who God is and what God offers, they see more clearly their own failures to respond in humility and gratitude. The saints see God's love more abundantly, and so they see their own sin all the more. They are examining their lives, not against worldly standards by which they appear good, but rather by the standard of God's perfect love revealed in Jesus Christ. And because the saints see their sin more distinctly, they marvel all the more at God's mercy.

Good Catholics sometimes tell me they don't know what to confess in the sacrament of reconciliation. "I don't do anything bad," they say. My first response, of course, is to remind them that sin is both a matter of what we have done but also of what we have left undone. Sin is both commission and omission. What good did I leave undone that I could have done? But more, we need to look deeply into our hearts to see the root of sin that lives within. There may be no external behaviors that others might judge to be wrong, but in our hearts we can still find our own selfishness, our lack of love and generosity, our failures truly to forgive, our harsh judgments of others, our lack of trust in God in the moments of difficulty and trial. How many of us can honestly say that we are focused sufficiently on our relationship with the Lord, given adequate time or effort to growing in communion with him, loved as selflessly as God has loved us in Jesus? In the end, we must ask ourselves if our failure to see the reality and the depth of sin isn't really a sign that we have not drawn close enough to the God of love to see the reality of our failures to love in return.

The sacrament of reconciliation, or confession, is a sacrament of conversion. We face the reality of our sin, and we encounter the undeserved mercy of God. In light of this mercy, we find new reason to be converted more deeply. We are renewed in our recognition of the wonder of God's invitation to us, and we are renewed in our decision to respond with our whole being.

Questions for Reflection

* *How do you experience sin in your own life? What are its roots in your heart?*

* *How do you think that "social sin" impacts your life and the lives of those you know?*

* *What is your image of God, and how does that image fit with your understanding of sin?*

* *When you think of Jesus as your Savior, from what do you picture him saving you?*

* *Why is it so difficult to surrender and trust in God?*

Prayer

Merciful and compassionate God, whose love is always greater than my sin, forgive and heal me. Forgive my sin, my failure to respond to your unimaginable invitation to enter into communion with you, my refusal to become what you have so wonderfully called and graced me to be. Too many, many times, I have said "no" to you and to those around me who are deserving of my love and attention. But I am confident in faith that you are always saying "Yes!" to sinners who want to return to you and begin again. And so am I at this moment, my God. I pray in the powerful name of my Savior, Jesus Christ, who is your mercy made flesh. Amen.

CHAPTER

IT IS FOR FREEDOM THAT CHRIST HAS SET US FREE

In the United States, we are justly proud of our freedom. It is one of the most basic values of our country. "Give me liberty or give me death," cried one of our nation's Founding Fathers. The fundamental rights that Americans hold most dear are often freedoms: free speech, freedom of religion, freedom to vote, freedom to assemble. Even in a society as violent as our own, the gun lobby has been able to appeal successfully to the right or freedom to bear arms, apparently protected with little restriction by our Constitution. Even the proponents of abortion in our society argue under the slogan "pro-choice"...pro-freedom. Who, in a society that holds freedom so dear, could possibly be opposed to a woman's personal freedom to choose? In our country, apparently, freedom is so nearly an absolute value that it trumps virtually every other value.

Freedom is our great value, and we undoubtedly enjoy many fundamental freedoms. But are we really free? Even with all the freedoms we enjoy and with all of the options available to us in our society, are we really basically and ultimately free? Do we really possess the freedom of which Saint Paul speaks when he says, "For freedom Christ has set us free" (Galatians 5:1)? Do we possess and live the freedom that Christ has won for us? In the end, did Jesus die for us just so we could have the freedom to vote, or to choose, or to bear arms?

In fact, in our society, which values freedom so dearly, we live in a world of addictions. At a practical and obvious level, we are not personally free. There are, of course, the well-known addictions for which there are helpful twelve-step programs: alcohol, drug, and pornography addictions. But whether we are addicted in one or more of these well-known ways or not, most of us are addicted to some degree in still other ways: to possessions, status, external appearances, human approval, control, power. In short, we are addicted to things that we mistakenly and tragically believe will give us security, make us happy, and fulfill us. Freely pursuing these things, we soon find ourselves enslaved by them.

Free to vote, free to buy whatever we can afford (or that our credit card limit will allow), free to bear deadly arms, and tragically free even to kill the unborn, we are at a more important and more fundamental level profoundly lacking in freedom. The truth is that the freedom for which Christ has set us free is the freedom to love God "with all our heart, all our soul...all our strength, all our mind...and our neighbor as ourselves." And who can honestly say that he or she loves with such totality? Yes, we want to love God and neighbor. And yes, perhaps we do so more or less consistently; but with all our hearts? And our neighbors as ourselves? If not, what stands in our way? Why can't we honestly say that we have arrived at such love? Well, yes, we are "only human." But the problem is really even more fundamental: our lack of true freedom, our love for and addiction to things that are less than God, our selfish love and concern for ourselves, and ultimately sin.

Freedom to Love, Freedom to Choose

Created in the image of God, who is love, we have been created with the fundamental freedom that alone makes love possible. Without freedom, there is no love. This basic freedom and the subsequent capacity to love are at the heart of what it means to be human. God created us with this freedom whose ultimate and true purpose is to respond freely in love and thus to "choose" God. The tragic but necessary consequence, however, is that we are also free to say "no" to God and to the divine self-offer. In the end, it has to be so. God respects the freedom given us. We are created in the image of a God who is love. Love is what God wants from us and for us. And we simply cannot love and truly be the image of God without freedom.

Obviously not every exercise of our freedom is directly and consciously about God. We make countless decisions, great and small, each day. But while many of them may seem completely inconsequential, in fact, each one is either a manifestation of our fundamental choice for God, confirming it and making it stronger, or that decision weakens, contradicts, and even reverses our decision to respond to God's self-offer.

Will I spend my money on this new trinket? Will I stop and lend a hand to my coworker at this moment? Will I take a moment to listen to that person's problem? Will I watch that particular program on television or visit that Web site on the Internet? Will I pass on what I just heard about that person? Will I slack off at work this afternoon? Will I give my child or spouse a few minutes of my precious time, when I feel so tired at this moment? In fact, in each small decision, whether consciously or not, I make myself to be a particular kind of person and, even more fundamentally, I choose how I will be before God, whether I will respond to God's love and conform myself to God's will at this moment, whether I will be what God calls and intends for me to be.

Again, it is true that not every decision is a conscious decision about my relationship with God. But in fact, conscious or not, every decision is related intrinsically to that relationship. In our exercise of freedom in ordinary choices, we make choices about ourselves and who we will be. And such choices simply cannot be separated from the more fundamental use of freedom for or against God; and, in the end, those are the only two options. In that sense, every moment of choice is a moment of judgment: Will I say "yes" to God or not? Will I respond to God's grace?

Freedom and Sin

As we saw in the previous chapter, the problem is sin. Sin impacts us at many interrelated levels. Sin—our own personal sin as well as the ways that sin has become embedded in our society—blinds us to the truth of what is truly good and important. God has given us a natural ability to know what is good, but sin clouds and blinds this ability. We do not see reliably that it is God we must choose, nor do we accurately see the good that ought to be done in order to conform ourselves to God and to the divine will. Sin causes blindness to what is good, and so, too, it deforms freedom's ability to choose the good.

Moreover, sin causes disorder in our desires. Our fundamental, inherent desire is for God and for the fulfillment that we can find only in God. At the same time, we have been created with many other desires; and in themselves, they are good. They are meant to direct and move us to those things and actions that will lead us to God, who is the source of all good and thus to our own authentic good as well. But because of sin, beginning with original sin and reinforced by what we see around us and our own history of sin, our desires become disordered, misdirected, and disproportionate. Rather than desiring what we should, as we should, we become focused on and even enslaved by things that are infinitely less than God or contrary to God's will. All of this is a new cause for blindness to what is truly good and a further source for the weakening and enslavement of our ability to choose rightly.

Sin infects the will as well. Our freedom is enslaved by these disordered desires, and our minds are blind to the truth of who we must choose in order to find our authentic security, fulfillment, pleasure, and happiness. Our freedom is burdened by our own history of sin and lured away by the bad example we see around us (and to which we sadly contribute). And so, even if, at one level, we truly desire God, want to respond to God's self-offer, and even sincerely decide to do so, because of sin we find ourselves unable to do so consistently, faithfully, and totally.

Obviously, sin is a contradiction of freedom's truest purpose. In fact, it is the tragic and utterly contradictory use of our freedom by which we act against what we are meant to be and to become. By sinning, we use what is most essential to our humanity to contradict what would make us most truly human—that is, the love of

God and neighbor lived out in our individual choices and actions. Thus it is true that in our society we value and enjoy various freedoms. But the sad reality is that, at the most fundamental level, we are profoundly unfree. Try to love faithfully and consistently, to place the needs of others above our own convenience, to overcome our habitual sin, and we discover all too quickly the depth of our lack of real freedom.

As Saint Paul says so clearly (Romans 6:6), we need to be set free from the slavery of sin. Our freedom needs to be set free. And this is precisely what Jesus has done. Through the cross and resurrection, we have been set free by Christ to love God and neighbor as we were created to do so that we can enter into communion with the triune God in Christ. In Christ, we are made free to truly decide to be Christian, to be his true and faithful disciples, following him along the path of unselfish, self-giving love that leads to eternal life.

While it is true that we are not completely free from the influence of sin and that the shaping of our freedom is a lifelong task, enabled by Christ's presence with us in the Spirit, the fundamental work of freeing our freedom is already accomplished in Christ. With the help of grace, we have to make it a consistent and deeper-lived reality in our lives.

"Purity of Heart"

Early monastic authors described the goal of our daily striving to be "purity of heart." Only the pure of heart can truly and freely love. Danish philosopher Søren Kierkegaard published a book of essays with the title *Purity of Heart Is to Will the One Thing*. To be truly free, to possess purity of heart, would mean to will our communion with God in response to God's gracious invitation and to will anything and everything else in keeping with and in light of this fundamental exercise of our freedom. A truly pure heart wills and chooses nothing apart from God.

True, unselfish love can only grow in a pure heart. Otherwise, our love will always be diluted, distracted, misdirected, obstructed, enslaved by selfishness, by self-centeredness, by sin.

Love fundamentally resides in the will, not in the emotions and feelings. This is another way of saying that, while the word "love" can be used to describe a feeling, love is most basically and truly a decision, a commitment. And decisions are made by consciously willing something in a stable way. Love, then, requires freedom. If we are truly to love God as God has commanded and as we must, if we are to become what we are truly meant to be, we must be fundamentally free. This is freedom's true and ultimate purpose: to allow us to live the great commandment to love God and neighbor totally, completely, eternally. Until we are free, until our hearts are truly pure, we can never truly and completely give ourselves to God and neighbor.

Jesus obviously possessed just such purity of heart. Led to his death and nailed to the cross, he was truly free—not physically, of course, in any of the ways that our society measures freedom—but profoundly and fully free. Confronted with all of the things that could make him focused on himself and tempt him to try to grasp control of the situation according to his own will, Jesus gave himself in love to the eternal Father, and he gave himself for the very people who brought him to his death. Jesus, nailed to the cross, was truly and profoundly free...while the people standing at the foot of cross (whether literally 2,000 years ago or figuratively here and now) were not profoundly free in the way that matters most. They were, rather, the slaves of their own ideas about God, their own priorities, their fears.

Choosing Freedom

"Deciding to be Christian"—this is the challenge we face today. We must each, consciously and for ourselves, decide we will be followers of Jesus Christ, that his values will be ours, that our priorities and choices will be based on what he teaches. This must be a conscious decision, a commitment, and a way of life. And so it is a decision that is really a fundamental life choice, a choice about how we will be in the world, about who we will be. It becomes the basis, then, of all of the rest of our choices; and all of the rest of our choices must increasingly be consistent with the fundamental disposition of our will. Such a decision and life commitment, then, must grow deeper and more consistent. We must integrate more and more all of our priorities and choices into it. We must wipe out any choice or value contrary to it. Or to say it in another way, we have to enter the path of ongoing conversion, the shaping of our freedom for an ever deeper and more consistent "yes" to God. We have to imitate Jesus' purity of heart. And, in the end, it is only life in Christ, participation in his Church, and openness to his power and mercy that can make this possible.

Questions for Reflection

* *In what ways are you unfree? How do you experience the pull, the attraction, or even the enslavement of sin?*

* *Recall Saint Ignatius' prayer, where he asks God to take his all: liberty, memory, understanding, will, and possessions. Through this well-known prayer, Ignatius reminds us that the Lord's love and grace are enough. If love is rooted in freedom, what does Ignatius mean by asking God to take his liberty?*

* *How can we grow in the freedom to love God more authentically?*

Prayer

God of my freedom, I make the sad words of Saint Paul my own: "I do not understand my own actions. For I do not do what I want, but I do the very thing I hate" (Romans 7:15). Feebly and inconsistently, I want to return your love and to live that love in my daily actions. But I am weak. And more, I find that, even when I want to do the right, I am pulled and held back, distracted and discouraged, by a power of selfishness that lives in me. Help me, my God! Free me, my Savior! Give me a truly pure heart so that I may faithfully love you and my brothers and sisters! In the name of Jesus, incarnate love, I pray. Amen.

7

THE STRUGGLE TO BE FREE

Take up your cross! Deny yourself! Sell what you have and give to the poor! All of these sayings of Jesus and more like them are familiar to us. But have we ever really stopped and asked ourselves if Jesus meant to be taken seriously? Do we take such challenges at face value? Or do we assume that Jesus was exaggerating, at least a bit, to make a point? Or is it that we would rather think so? What if Jesus intended to be taken, if not literally, still quite seriously, without exaggeration? After all, he himself took up the cross. He denied himself. He gave himself completely for the sake of poor sinners like us. More, all of the great saints have done so, too, each in his or her own way. But not us? Can we really be his true followers, his faithful disciples, and refuse to follow him on the way of the cross?

In fact, the cross is the path to freedom. In this world of sin, it is the only path to the true freedom that Jesus came to bring. As we have seen, it is sin that corrupts our freedom and thus our ability truly and faithfully to love God and neighbor. Left on our own, it would be impossible for us to free ourselves from the slavery of sin that is the human condition apart from Christ.

But the cross of Jesus changes everything. The death of the crucified Jesus was the moment of encounter between the infinite love of God and the power of sin. In his humanity, Jesus took on the burden of our sin, the history of our refusals of God's love, and he freely chose to surrender to the Father and to his will. Truly free, pure of heart, Jesus said "yes" to the Father. And thus he destroyed the power of sin, showed us the way, and made it possible for us to say our own "yes" to the Father in the freedom that God has given to each of us. We must therefore follow Jesus on the way of surrender to the Father's love; and because of our sin, we must learn freedom through the experience and the power of the cross. We cannot arrive at this freedom truly to decide to be a follower of Jesus, to love God and our neighbor as Jesus has taught, unless we follow him on that path, even as he himself told his disciples so clearly: "If any want to become my followers, let them deny themselves and take up their cross daily and follow me" (Luke 9:23). See also Matthew 10:38; 16:24; Mark 8:34; Luke 14:27.

In the next chapter, I want to look at the cross of suffering and of acceptance, a cross that confronts us and that we must ultimately choose to embrace. Here I want to speak of the same cross, but in a form that, with God's help, we must actively and consciously pursue.

Asceticism

Self-denial...self-discipline...these are the root meanings of the word "asceticism." The Christian life requires asceticism, ascetical discipline and practice, just as an athlete needs to train, to exercise, to work to develop discipline and skill to attain goals. The Christian life is not easy. The attainment of the freedom that Jesus wants to give us is a path of discipline and even struggle, carried on with God's help.

We don't talk much about asceticism these days. If we think about it at all, we might associate it with what we give up for Lent. And yet, asceticism in the form of sacrifice, self-denial, and the basic effort to overcome vice and develop virtue has always been seen in the Christian tradition as essential to serious growth in the life of faith. Perhaps it has passed into relative obscurity because many forms of Christian asceticism had become misguided or disconnected from their more positive purpose as tools in the empowerment of freedom. At the same time, human nature being what it is and being sinners as we are, perhaps we have been quite content to leave aside the reminder of the need for discipline and sacrifice in our lives. Certainly, in a world of consumerism and instant gratification, asceticism seems foolish or old-fashioned.

Ascetical practice has no value in itself. It is an instrument, a path to be followed to reach a goal. We want to surrender ourselves to God, truly to choose the path that leads to divine communion, to attain that freedom that makes it possible. But we are sinners, burdened by the reality and history of our own sin and by our involvement in the sin around us that blinds us, disorders our desires, and hinders our freedom. Yes, Jesus is our sure guide, and he has sent the Holy Spirit to empower us to attain this goal. But our communion with God requires our effort in cooperation with grace. And this is the basic, positive meaning and purpose of Christian asceticism.

We can speak of asceticism as a parallel to the practice of athletes. We shape our freedom for the good by training. We deny ourselves, for a time, even good things so we can empower ourselves to deny ourselves the bad. We strengthen ourselves against the temptation to sin by learning to deny ourselves good things that we want at this moment. We refuse ourselves the instant gratification of our desires so we can resist when the temptation to sin comes along. Authentic asceticism in this form, of course, does not do anything that would harm our health, which is a God-given good and responsibility. But fasting for a time, denying ourselves television, Internet access, or certain types of food can be good for us, both spiritually and physically—just as the self-denial and hard work of the athlete prepares him or her to attain the goal, to win the game.

We all know that such ascetical practice can be difficult. In that sense, it is a share in the cross through which we seek to develop and strengthen that fundamental freedom by which we hope, more consistently and more deeply, to say "yes" to God.

Overcoming Sin and Vice

The most basic and first step of asceticism is the effort to stop committing sin. Overcoming the sin that plagues our daily lives requires its own intentional, graced effort, as we know from experience. For some of us, this means the effort to overcome some grave sin. For others, it is sin that is perhaps less serious but just as persistent, such as a habit of gossip or uncharitable remarks about others.

These sins must be faced directly, and the traditional counsel is still valid: We must do our best to avoid situations and people that are "near occasions of sin." At times, it can be helpful to try to discover, within ourselves, the inner attraction of our own particular sins, to gain insight into our sin. At the same time, we must join our own efforts to overcome sin to the work of prayer, a habit of prayer, and specific prayer in time of temptation. Our broader effort at discipline and self-denial can also be a help in taming a particular sin. More subtly perhaps, it was commonplace of early monastic authors to suggest that the root for one sin may actually be found in other sins. Attacking the root of one sin may relieve the temptation to another. Attention to gluttony and anger, for example, can be a help against lust.

The deeper problem of overcoming sin is that sin so easily becomes a habit. A particular sin becomes our "default mode." We don't just fall into sin in individual situations that are unrelated to one another. Often we do so because we have developed habits of sinning in that way. Gossiping, for instance, fits into a broader pattern of needlessly passing on what one hears about others—perhaps, for example, to enhance one's standing in a group as the one who is "in the know." Each individual act of sin reinforces that pattern so it will be even easier the next time an opportunity to gossip comes along. It will be that much harder to resist the temptation. We call such bad habits "vices." A vice is the habitual tendency to some bad action that is built up over time by practice. And so, the real focus of our struggle is not just individual moments of temptation but the vices that are at their root.

This explains why we can go to confession, be absolved of our sin, be filled with God's grace, and yet still find it so hard to resist the very same sin as soon as we walk out of the reconciliation room. Yes, we have been forgiven. Yes, God is giving us the grace to do better. But at the same time, the vice still lives in us; we have not yet uprooted the bad habit that we have built up over time. While there is reason for hope, there is also clear reason for focused effort and discipline. We must continue to call out for grace and frequent the sacraments, but we must also work to uproot the bad habits that burden us and weigh us down.

The vices are the negative shaping of our freedom away from God. We may *want* to say "yes" to God. We may *intend* to be true followers of Jesus. But the presence of vices in our lives means our freedom is shaped and formed to move us away from him. We need God's help. And, with his grace, we need to get to work!

Growing in Virtue

The more positive form of this basic Christian asceticism is the effort to grow in virtues, that is, the good habits that are the opposite of vices. We want to be able to do the good, not just occasionally or by chance, but regularly and consistently. We want to do so without having to struggle each time to overcome contrary temptations. This means that we must develop virtues, habitual tendencies to do the good. Doing the good must become our "default mode." These good habits are built over time by our (graced) efforts that empower us to do the good consistently, without struggle. In this way, our freedom is formed, strengthening and deepening our ability to freely love God and neighbor.

The virtue of honesty, for example, is built up by telling the truth in one situation after another, even though it may seem more convenient at the time to tell a "little white lie." It is built up by refusing one temptation to tell one lie after another, and by picking ourselves up after each slip and deciding, with God's help, to do better. Once we have developed the virtue of honesty, we can more easily tell the truth in the face of a serious temptation to lie or to evade the truth for some selfish reason.

The work of virtue-building is not easy. It takes time and effort, hand-in-hand with prayer and participation in the life of the sacraments. But it is the path of developing, strengthening, and truly empowering our freedom in a fundamental way.

The virtues are learned and formed not just in this ascetical way, essential though it may be. We learn Christian virtues, the habitual tendencies and attitudes that we ought to have, precisely by entering more deeply into the Christian vision of life. We learn from Jesus the basic attitudes and priorities that we ought to have in life. We learn by reading his teaching and observing his example in the Gospels. But we take it in, absorb it even more deeply, by entering into the story of Jesus by entering personally, prayerfully, meditatively into the Gospel stories. In the Gospels we encounter not just stories *about* Jesus, we encounter the Lord Jesus and learn from him. Those who regularly pray over the Scriptures or who meditate on the life of Jesus, for example in the mysteries of the rosary, breathe in the basic attitudes and priorities of Jesus. Who could, for example, pray daily over the Gospels and not at least feel the need and desire to grow in generosity toward others, a spirit of forgiveness, humility, a zeal to attend to those who are outcast?

And more, the virtues are learned and developed by entering more deeply into the sacramental and liturgical life of the Church. In doing so, we encounter the Lord. The celebration of the Eucharist, for example, in which strangers come together as brothers and sisters to break bread, is meant to form in us fundamental attitudes of equality, reconciliation, and sharing. The sacrament of reconciliation, especially when celebrated in common, develops in us an attitude of mutual forgiveness and support in Christian living. The celebration of Christian marriage draws all of us, not only the married couple, into the spirit of generous self-giving, which is the attitude of Christ in relationship to his bride, the Church.

The saints also teach us the life of virtue. Recalling their memory in our personal devotions and in the Church's liturgical calendar draws us into their virtuous lives, often in more specific ways. The popular image of Saint Francis of Assisi moves us to a greater reverence for creation and a spirit of simplicity. A deeper understanding of his life and teaching moves us to a life of humble surrender to God and commitment to prayer. In the contemporary world, many Christians have been moved by the example of Blessed Mother Teresa to action on behalf of those in need. The heroic ministry of Saint Damian of Molokai to lepers can move us to reach out to outcasts and to those at the margins of society. Saint Thérèse, the Little Flower, offers an example of holiness and the vocation to love, lived out in the ordinary. The examples and possibilities to be formed in virtues by meditation of the lives of the saints are endless.

Virtues grow in us through our own effort over time, aided by grace. Virtues grow by our entering more deeply into the life of Christ, by meditating more deeply on the whole of the Scriptures, by participating more attentively to the liturgy and sacraments, by celebrating the life and memory of the saints. But most fundamentally and essentially, virtues grow in us because we allow God's grace to accomplish this good in us. God is always at work so that we can truly learn to love as God has so wondrously loved us.

Conscience, our ability to discern the good to be done, works hand-in-hand with our freedom. It is formed in a similar way to the virtues. Yes, we form our consciences by learning about right and wrong, learning what the Church teaches about particular moral questions, gaining knowledge about what is truly good, and developing a keener sense of what is truly valuable in a sometimes morally confused and confusing world. But we also form our consciences as we form our freedom in virtue by developing an authentically Christian vision of ourselves and the world, by participating and allowing ourselves to be formed by the sacramental life of the Church, by recalling with devotion the lives of the saints, and in the prayer by which we allow God to form our ability to know and to choose what is truly good in love.

God's Grace Invites Us to Freedom

God is always pouring grace upon us. The Holy Spirit is always at work. More than we could ever wish, God wants to form our freedom so that we can give our lives freely in return. At times, we may feel as if all the work to overcome sin, uproot vice, and develop virtues is ours. In fact, even the slightest effort on our part would be impossible without the mighty help of God. We could not begin this work, sustain it, or bring it to fruition without divine help at every step. And it is for this reason that ascetical practice and prayer must always go hand-in-hand. They are partners in the Christian life, in the path that leads to freedom and thus to communion.

Saint Thomas Aquinas taught that "love is the form of the virtues"—which is to say that love is meant to shape, fill, and empower all of our attitudes and actions. Love of God and neighbor become the driving force of all of our virtues, of every choice and action. Thus, the sometimes hard, always grace-filled effort to grow in virtue strengthens our freedom so we can truly love. At the same time, a deepening love of God draws together all of our desires and choices so we can more fully love as God first loved us.

Questions for Reflection

* *Have you tried any particular ascetical practices? If so, why those?*

* *Can you identify in yourself the roots/causes of your typical sins?*

* *What vice(s) do you need to overcome now in order to be more truly free?*

* *What virtue(s) have you worked to develop in your life? Which virtue(s) do you need most to develop now?*

* *What are the most distinctive attitudes and virtues that we can learn from the example and teaching of Jesus in the Gospels?*

* *Are there particular saints who inspire you to grow in specific virtues?*

Prayer

God of my strength, in my mind I know that to love you is my truest fulfillment, and to love you truly is my deepest desire. At this moment you are inviting me and gracing me to enter into the heart of your love for me. Empower me by your heavenly aid to embrace the cross that leads to freedom, to enter the struggle, to claim the grace to attain so wonderful a treasure. Liberate my freedom so that I may love you in action and with a firm and consistent resolve. In the name of Jesus, my true and only liberator, I pray. Amen.

THE CROSS AND THE "DARK FAITH" OF THE MATURE CHRISTIAN

Saint Thomas à Kempis, in his medieval devotional classic, *The Imitation of Christ*, has a powerful chapter titled "The Royal Road of the Cross." There, he observes that we Christians typically and all too easily say that we want to be followers of Jesus. "I want to follow Jesus!" "I will follow Jesus wherever he leads me"...*until*, that is, his way leads to the cross, as inevitably it does. Christ always leads us to the cross. In fact, we could say that ordinary human existence leads us inexorably to the cross, that is, to moments or periods of suffering, disappointment, loss of control, and death. No matter what we make ourselves to be in life or what we have accumulated, eventually we will find ourselves facing a difficulty we cannot surmount with everything that we have at our disposal. If nothing else, it will be the unavoidable reality of death.

In this sense, all of humankind comes inevitably to confront the cross. The question that Jesus really asks us is: Will you accept the cross? Will you embrace the cross? Will you take up the cross in faith, in a spirit of surrender, with trust in the Father's love and presence, as I did? The real question for us to answer is: Will we embrace the cross in our lives and follow the crucified one along the way of faith, hope, and love? Or will we allow ourselves to become bitter, angry, turned in on ourselves...or seek escape from the inescapable cross through some selfish diversion...or medicate ourselves in one of many possible ways in order to deaden ourselves to the painful and unavoidable reality of the cross?

Today there are some who try to preach a gospel that suggests that if we are really faithful or at least if we pray hard enough or in just the right way, Christ ensures that our lives will be free of suffering. This gospel is false. All we have to do is live long enough to have it proven wrong. We are often tempted to think that if we remain in our difficulty even after sincere prayer, then there must be something wrong with God, who has somehow failed to see what we really need. The simple fact is that faith in Christ does not bring us freedom from suffering. His own life was not free from suffering, nor was the life of his Blessed Mother, nor the lives of the saints. How could we possibly think that the life of his followers would be free of suffering? What Christian faith ultimately offers us is not immunity from suffering but rather peace in the midst of trial, a deeper sense of joy in possessing something more important and enduring, a sense of hope that there is a greater good beyond this present difficulty.

Yes, we must pray in faith. Yes, we must ask for what we believe we need. Yes, we must believe in the power of prayer. But ultimately, faith is trust in the wisdom and the loving will of God in the face of suffering that is not relieved even after real and persevering prayer. Faith at its deepest level is the faith of Jesus on the cross, abandoning himself completely to the Father even as he cried out, "My God, my God, why have you forsaken me?" (Matthew 27:46).

In the previous chapter, we reflected on the reality of the cross in a form in which, at least in a sense, we choose for ourselves. We freely embrace the struggle of a true asceticism in order to know the liberty that Jesus has won for us. In this chapter, we are looking at the cross, not in a form that is chosen, but as we find it looming ahead of us uninvited, as it is dropped into our laps, in the form of life's inevitable and unavoidable suffering, loss, disappointments, failures, sickness, and finally death, our own and that of those we love.

Personally, I don't believe we can arrive at a mature Christian faith until we've suffered, until we've been confronted by difficulties and losses that cannot be alleviated by human effort or through the power of prayer. In such situations and times, we are forced to decide whether we will, in fact, embrace the cross in faith or try to run from it. Before this critical crossroads, we can learn *about* the faith; we can have the faith of a child. Faith, yes, but not a *mature* faith, not a faith that has looked into the heart of the real demands of Christian living, which is always a way of the cross, leading to the resurrection. It is no accident that the cross is the central image of our faith. The cross is the symbol of what God has done for us in Christ's death and resurrection, and it is the road map that we must follow in our lives.

Let's be clear. The God of Jesus Christ does not will our suffering for its own sake. God is a God of infinite love. God wills only our good. Jesus in his earthly existence healed the sick, reached out to the poor, and raised the dead. To the degree that we can follow him in relieving the suffering of others—and even our own—we should strive to do so. But God does permit suffering. And, in a world of sin, it is the path that can lead us to freedom—depending, of course, on how we confront it. As the death and resurrection definitively show us, God brings unimagined good from the suffering of those who are willing to wait in trust for God's love to transform death into newness of life.

In our human existence, we all know the experience of having grown from facing the difficulties that we would have hoped to avoid. We find ourselves stronger or wiser or more seasoned by what we endured. As the old saying goes, "Whatever doesn't kill us makes us stronger." In that sense, life itself—and ultimately faith—is like athletic preparation: We grow through endurance and perseverance.

In my pastoral ministry, I have seen time and again how important faith can be in moments of serious illness, death, and grief. Faith in God's unseen presence, hope in a better future, trust that God will see us through this present difficulty all make such a difference in times of struggle. Generally, when you walk into a funeral home to visit a grieving family, you'll see the tears and feel the sadness. When you walk into a patient's room in the hospital critical care unit or emergency room, you'll encounter the anxiety, worry, and the sense of impending loss. This is true whether those you encounter are people of faith or not. Being a disciple of Jesus does not free one from this fundamental human reality. And still, what a difference faith makes!

What a difference it makes when the grieving spouse and family believe in the resurrection, when there is faith that somehow God is present in this tragic situation, when there is trust that somehow God will see them through even though it does not feel possible in this moment. What a difference faith makes in seeing us through the difficulties of life. The truth that I want to highlight here is how faith can grow precisely through these hard times as we do our best to hold on to it, to go on believing, to surrender in trust in the face of what is happening to us or to those we love.

Often more difficult than our own suffering is walking with our loved ones in their illness, decline, and death. We pray that they might be freed from this difficulty. We pray for healing over and over again, that impending death will be turned back. We call on others to join us in heartfelt prayer. We bargain, we promise, we plead. Yet nothing changes. Our loved one goes on suffering, dying. Our loved one dies, too young, too unexpectedly, so undeservedly. At a moment such as this, our faith can be shaken to its very core. But at the same time, rarely is there such an opportunity, such an invitation, to embrace the cross, to surrender to God's will, and so to draw close to Christ on the cross. Many times, in the midst of the situation, we find that we can do so, only halfheartedly, reluctantly, or imperfectly. And yet God makes our faith grow, though we may only discover it later.

The simple fact is that, in this life, we don't have to look for the cross. We don't have to try to find one. Yes, we can profitably select for ourselves the sacrifices and self-denials by which we can exercise our growth into true freedom, abstaining from or denying ourselves this or that. But the real cross, fitted uniquely to our personal shoulder, is usually found looming, unwanted, before us. Paradoxically, but truly and profoundly, our true freedom lies in embracing the cross, in surrender, in trusting acceptance.

There is great wisdom in the well-known "Serenity Prayer" of Protestant theologian Reinhold Niebuhr:

God, grant me the serenity
To accept the things I cannot change,
Courage to change the things I can,
And the wisdom to know the difference.

The Cross of Acceptance

In this chapter, we have been reflecting on the cross of suffering. In the previous chapter, we looked at the cross of asceticism. But there is another typical human experience that invites us to embrace the cross by surrendering and thus growing in faith and freedom. This often arises in the form of the "midlife crisis"; less dramatic perhaps for most of us, and yet no less profound in its invitation and opportunity.

When we're young, life can seem full of endless possibilities. Countless options lie before us. We can do this or that. We can become what we will—even things that we have not yet imagined. Prince Charming or Ms. Right will come along, if we just wait. We will eventually have what we presently lack. We will always succeed in what we set out to do.

However, with the passing of the years and decades, we come to realize that life simply doesn't always work that way. We don't always succeed at what we set out to do. We don't always find the idyllic, perfect mate. Or we achieve or gain what we want and find that, in the end, it doesn't really satisfy. By the time we awaken to midlife existence, we find we are not exactly where or who we hoped to be, or we realize that our "ultimate" goal was not worthy of the hope that we placed in it.

This is the midlife crisis, or a typical form that it takes. By midlife, after years of struggling to attain our goals, trying out the options available to us, banging our heads against the obstacles that stand in our way, we are forced to stop, take stock, and reevaluate. It can be a period of real soul-searching, dissatisfaction, and discontent. Some strike out to try again to realize their youthful dreams in a dramatic way: the stereotypical little red sports car, the "new and trendy look," or a new relationship more akin to our fantasies than to our realities.

The spiritual life has its own parallel. When we become serious about the faith, especially when we are filled with the idealistic enthusiasm of the young, we set out to become saints. Although intellectually we may know better, we feel that for us the path will be easy, direct, and brief. But again, we find that it just isn't so. The path to sanctity is long and hard, full of stops and starts. Inevitably and regularly, we are confronted with our own weakness, our sin, our natural lethargy. Although the journey may start out with sweet feelings and seemingly profound experiences, prayer is hard. Sustaining a life of prayer takes effort and discipline. Prayer unavoidably passes through times, sometimes long periods, of dryness.

High ideals are necessary and wonderful. The enthusiasm and energy of youth is something we sometimes long to reclaim. But authentic ideals cannot exist independent of reality, of the real stuff of human existence. Disappointing though it might be at first, pulling our heads out of the clouds to look squarely at the reality of who we are, the path we must walk, and the real distance to the goal is the only authentic way to finally arrive at the goal. In fact, midlife is an invitation to accept and embrace reality, to surrender to it—or really, to surrender to God's will in the midst of the world and life as we find it. Then we can really decide to be Christian because we see ourselves, our world, and the real path ahead of us as they really are.

At midlife, we can finally accept life as it is. We can accept the cards we've been dealt in life. We can accept our history, what happened to us in the past, both the happy and tragic moments, and what we did or didn't do that can't be undone. And we can find that it's OK. I'm OK. And having accepted reality as it is, we can finally look around at the world as it is, at our past as it was, and see the blessings that are actually there to be seen. Too often, though, we ignore the blessings because we have been looking elsewhere, our heads in the clouds, our eyes on a goal that is unattainable without sure footing in the present reality. We can see the good things, the people, the relationships as imperfect but good. My life will not be exactly as I had dreamed. And that's OK. My past cannot be undone. And it's OK.

In the spiritual life, too, I can accept that I really am a sinner in need of God's mercy—really, and that's not a pious slogan. I can really and humbly appeal to that superabundant divine mercy. I can accept that the spiritual journey is long and at times arduous. And that's OK. My prayer is as it is, more ordinary and more at its beginning than I had hoped for myself at this point. The path to the deeper, sustained prayer that I sincerely desire will be long and, at times, dry and seemingly unfruitful. And that's OK, too. Spiritually, I am as I am. And that's OK. It's OK with me. And, more importantly, though God wants to give me so much more, it's OK with God, too.

I am not talking about pessimism. I am not advocating the abandonment of our ideals and goals. I'm not talking about stepping back from the journey to our truest self, which is oneself in deep communion with God. I am talking about a liberating acceptance—acceptance of life as it is, ourselves as we are, our fundamental, God-given and God-blessed humanity. Then and only then can we truly decide and set out along the real path to the attainment, with God's help, of life's truest goal.

The Cross of Prayer

We are reflecting on the power of the cross to set us free to truly decide to be Christian in its deepest sense: by the cross of ascetical practice, of suffering, of acceptance. The life of prayer, too, brings the cross in a number of ways. While the next chapter focuses on prayer, here I want to focus on prayer precisely as a share in the cross. Prayer is a discipline. While we may enjoy moments when prayer brings intense feelings of joy, comfort, and the sense of divine presence, it is just as likely that there will be even more times of dryness in prayer when we don't particularly feel like praying and don't feel good in or about our prayer.

The great spiritual teachers of our tradition have taught us that, perhaps paradoxically, dry prayer can be the best prayer. God works at a level far deeper than our feelings and even than our thoughts. If we do our best to open ourselves to God in a time of prayer, even if we find ourselves distracted or dry, we can be sure that God remains at work, that we can truly encounter the divine presence. The reality of what is happening in prayer may not be apparent to us at that moment, but it will surely bear fruit later, for prayer is always fruitful when we trust in God.

This reality reminds us of the truth that authentic prayer cannot be judged by how it feels. In our world of instant gratification, in an age that seeks experiences and good feelings, we are easily fooled into thinking that we must always be seeking good experiences in prayer, that "good" prayer is prayer in which we feel the divine presence. When our prayer, then, does not feel good, there must be something wrong with the way we are praying. That may be the case, or it may just be that we are experiencing an inevitable time of dryness in prayer. Our job is to keep our "noses to the grindstone" and remain faithful to the discipline of prayer. God's presence and our mutual encounter in prayer may or may not flow out into a felt presence. In fact, most of us know from experience that if our prayer depended on our feelings we wouldn't persevere in prayer for long.

Dry prayer can be the best prayer because it teaches us the discipline of prayer. It instructs us how to deepen our trust in God's grace rather than primarily in our own efforts. Dryness helps us develop a real habit of prayer that can sustain us through prolonged periods of aridity and permit us to wait for God to be manifested as God wills. Dry prayer bears fruit as time and effort is offered freely to God without a felt reward for the person praying. Saint Francis de Sales cautions us that we must desire the God of consolations, not the consolations of God (*Introduction to the Devout Life*, 4.13). It must be God that we desire and not the superficial feelings of peace or joy that we might receive in prayer. Saint John of the Cross teaches us that we must not allow ourselves to become "spiritual gluttons," hungering, not for God, but for one good spiritual experience after another (*The Dark Night*, I, 6).

The life of prayer is an ascetical sharing in the cross, a carrying of the cross, that is both part of our decision to follow after Jesus into the life of the Trinity and one that brings us a deeper surrender to God as God truly is rather than just what we superficially want.

Dark Faith and the Dark Night

The cross in our life, in whatever form it takes, leads us into a deeper, more mature faith. We come to see that real faith is ultimately a "dark" faith, that is, a faith that does not have to see in order to believe, to feel in order to follow, to be affirmed tangibly in order to go on.

So often we think of faith as what we think we know about God and God's ways, of what we can be assured, what we can believe in confidence. Fair enough. But the cross points us to a different, deeper, essential aspect of faith—a dark faith, the sustained belief and surrender in the face of what we cannot know or see or understand. In faith, ultimately, we must learn to walk with Jesus, to follow him to the cross where he did not see, understand, or feel the Father's presence. Even as he said, "My God, my God, why have you forsaken me?" Jesus went on believing.

The cross in our lives teaches us precisely this deep and mature faith. Embraced, it transforms our faith from a child's faith to a mature and adult faith. It teaches us the true meaning of the cross as a path to resurrection, to rebirth, and to newness of life. It allows us to embrace the Christian life with our eyes open and our hearts ready. And so, as Jesus has already shown us, the cross is a symbol of victory. The cross is the passage to new and true life. The cross is the path—the only path—to the true and fundamental freedom by which we decide to be Christ's true followers along the way that leads to eternal communion with the triune God.

Ultimately, we want to be able to say boldly with Saint Paul: "I have been crucified with Christ; and it is no longer I who live, but it is Christ who lives in me. And the life I now live in the flesh I live by faith in the Son of God, who loved me and gave himself for me" (Galatians 2:19–20).

Questions for Reflection

* *How have you encountered the cross in your life? How did you respond? How did you grow?*

* *Have you encountered Christians whom it seemed to you embraced their personal cross with a spirit of faith and acceptance?*

* *What in your past and in your present challenges you to a deeper degree of acceptance?*

* *How do you respond to dryness in prayer? What would you advise others?*

* *How have you felt the challenge to walk in a "dark faith?"*

Prayer

Infinite and transcendent God, beyond the power of my mind to grasp, your ways are beyond me, your will always a loving mystery to me. Guide me to walk in a dark faith that trusts when it cannot understand, that accepts what it cannot change, that surrenders in the face of hardships that it cannot overcome, and that continues always to love as did Jesus, my Lord, on his saving cross. In his blessed and holy name I pray. Amen.

9

PRAYER IN TRUST AND SURRENDER

God calls sinners into relationship, into divine communion. Of course, an essential part of this communion is prayer. The Good News invites us to respond. In the moral life, we strive, with God's help, to become the kind of people and to act in the way that makes us most authentically who and what we were meant to be. We thereby fulfill the divine will and follow the path that leads us to God. In prayer, we draw close to God in response to this same Good News and invitation. In both, we form and shape our freedom, seek to overcome sin, and strengthen our life decision to be a follower of Christ.

Prayer has and can be defined in many ways. For our purposes here, we don't need to settle on one precise definition. Rather, we can look briefly at a few ways of understanding prayer that help us to see the progression that is possible and necessary in the authentic life of prayer.

We have all experienced prayer as "talking with God." Whether we are saying established prayers out of a prayer book, from memory, or speaking to God silently in our minds about our needs, we can say that prayer has this character of communication with God. The danger is that we are doing all of the talking and none of the listening. Prayer should be a conversation *with* God, not just talking *at* God. Perhaps we will never hear God speaking to us in a concrete form. But God does speak to us in the quiet, frequently even without words. Sometimes we only realize later what it is that God is communicating to us, outside of our formal time of prayer, as we suddenly find that we have new insight. This depends on listening as well as speaking.

Furthermore, prayer has been defined as "raising our minds and hearts to God," and this definition takes a step beyond simply talking with God or at least reveals more clearly the context of all true prayer. We see that prayer is more than thinking about God and more than conscious and explicit talking with God. In fact, prayer is holistic, a matter of mind and heart, thought and feeling, attentiveness and presence. This deeper understanding helps us to see that prayer can be done anywhere, since we can always raise our hearts and minds to God—in church, outside on a beautiful day, while driving, or sitting in the busy waiting room of a hospital's emergency department.

At a deeper level still, though consistent with what we have already said, we can say prayer is a "being with God," being open and attentive to God's presence with us and within us. As our prayer grows more mature and deepens—as our relationship with God matures and grows—our prayer becomes increasingly wordless, it becomes less talkative and more an experience of the presence of God. This type of prayer is often referred to as contemplative, which is the natural progression of deepening prayer to which all are called. This is not to say that we can all expect to experience visions or other special spiritual phenomena. But God invites all of us to enter into silent communion in the intimacy of a friendship that does not require words or talking of any sort.

Mature prayer is also habitual prayer. It is consistent. It is part of life and not just an occasional activity that we engage in when we feel like it, when we need something in particular, or when we can manage to fit it in. This is to say that prayer is part of our fundamental life commitment to enter into a sustained and deepening relationship with God in Christ.

Much more could be said profitably about prayer, but there are many fine books on prayer to which we can turn. My purpose here is more modest, to insist that prayer is an essential part of the Christian life and commitment and that it is a necessary part of our growth in true freedom when we say "yes" to God.

Presuppositions About Prayer

There are certainly various ways to define or understand prayer, and our experience of prayer changes over time. But in order to truly understand prayer as a part of our life decision to follow Christ and to answer God's invitation into relationship, it may be helpful to place prayer in a broader and more fundamental context. In fact, I want to suggest four presuppositions about what prayer is and how it fits into our Christian discipleship. What follows is not a "how to" about prayer but a discussion of what prayer fundamentally is.

1. OUR RESPONSE TO THE GOOD NEWS

As we have seen, our faith in Jesus Christ and our lives as Christians are grounded first and foremost in the Good News. Almighty God loves sinners! God loves us just as we are. And we, all of us, are sinners. The true life of faith begins with recognizing, accepting, and embracing *this* Good News.

Almighty God loves sinners...and God invites these sinners into relationship. God invites us, mere creatures and sinners, into friendship and intimate communion. God invites us to participate in divine life and love. Sometimes we should stop and marvel at the wonder of this Good News and the amazing invitation that God extends to us.

Our prayer can only truly be understood within the context of this invitation and our response. Prayer is an essential part, along with our moral living, of our acceptance of God's invitation. Prayer is our response to God's invitation to enter into ever-deepening relationship, both in a general way and in each moment of prayer.

Prayer is possible because God invites us into communion. This is true in a general and fundamental way—God invites us into a sustained friendship that is meant to grow deeper and broader—but it is also true for every moment of prayer. In faith, we know that we are not capable of any good action without the help of grace. Any good that we truly choose to do as human beings is the result of our cooperation with God's grace. Every time we feel moved to pray or manage to rise above our laziness or to pull ourselves away from our many activities in order to pray, it is because God has invited us, because God has touched us with grace, because God has renewed the graced invitation to this sinner. The fact is that God wants to make intimate friends with each one of us. God doesn't want us to be just people who believe in an abstract, impersonal way. God doesn't want us to be mere acquaintances who chat when we happen to encounter one another or who "talk from time to time." God wants intimate friendship with us, and prayer is a central part of this relationship and its growth and deepening.

And, like any human friendship, our relationship with God can and must deepen. This is a matter of spending more time in prayer, as our state in life permits; but it is even more a matter of opening ourselves more intimately and deeply to the divine presence. God is infinite. Our desire for God is infinite, and our need for God, too, is infinite. To be human is to be an infinite capacity for an infinite God. And so our prayer can always—and must always—grow deeper.

As we enter into any relationship, and this is especially true in our relationship with God, the experience of the person or persons will grow ever deeper and richer.

That prayer is central to our response to Good News tells us where prayer begins. Along what path does it lead us?

2. Our Surrender to God in Trust

In order truly to understand prayer, it is essential to see that the goal of our lives as Christians, indeed as human beings created in the image of God, is simply trust in and surrender to God in union with Christ in his surrender on the cross.

It is no accident that the central image of our faith as Christians is the cross of Jesus Christ. It is the essential symbol of our faith because it reveals the wondrous reality of God's love for us and how we are saved by the death of the Son of God. It is no less the central image of our faith because it lays out before us the path that we must walk. Jesus says as much when he tells us in the Gospels that we must take up the cross and follow him. To follow Jesus always means joining him in surrendering our lives to the Father, as Jesus did—discovering God's will, accepting God's will, doing God's will. We must do likewise, trusting that the divine will for us and for the world, even when mysterious to us, is always a loving will. We must trust that God is always willing a greater good for us, despite the difficulties that confront us, just as Jesus trusted and ultimately experienced the unimagined good of the resurrection that flowed from his cross.

Our prayer is always an essential part of this broader task of surrender. Traditionally, it has been said that there are four broad types of prayer: petition, repentance, thanksgiving, and adoration. I want to suggest that all four types can be understood in the context of surrender and trust.

In petition, we ask God for something that we believe we need for ourselves or for others. Sadly, for many of us, this is often our most frequent, even nearly exclusive form of prayer: "God, give me something." But when we offer a prayer of petition to God with a truly Christian attitude, we always do so humbly. We always acknowledge that God's wisdom and love for us and for those for whom we petition are always greater than our own. And so, while we may really want and really believe that what we ask for is utterly essential to us at this particular moment, in the end, in faith, we are always placing our petitions into God's provident hand. We are always humbly giving our need over to God in surrender and trust. All prayers of supplication are ultimately a form of surrender and trust.

In repentance, we are humbly acknowledging our sin and our need for God's mercy and renewing grace. We humbly ask for forgiveness and for an ability to change—two things that we cannot grant ourselves. In asking for God's mercy, we are always acknowledging that the divine mercy is an undeserved gift. In that sense, we are always "throwing ourselves on God's mercy." To ask for God's forgiveness is to give ourselves, just as we are, over to God with humble and grateful trust in his mercy and in a renewed surrender to him. In thanksgiving, we are acknowledging that the good things we have come from God, who is truly the source of every blessing and of every good gift. And so, in expressing our gratitude to God, we are renewing our trust in this bountiful divine love for us. In acknowledging God as the source of all good, we are humbly admitting once again that we need God, and we are thereby renewing our surrender, in both good times and bad. This is one reason that regular and sustained prayer of gratitude can help to see us through difficult times. Our recognition of God's goodness to us and our prayer of gratitude form within us that spirit of trust in God that helps us to trust in the divine presence when we face hardships in life.

In adoration, we acknowledge who and what God truly is: transcendent, infinite love, and goodness. In prayer of adoration, we place ourselves humbly before God as we are, acknowledging the wonder of who it is who invites us into this divine presence. This is the experience of Moses, who took off his shoes and hid his face in the presence of God ("I am who I am") in the form of the burning bush (Exodus 3:1–6). These are the experiences of the Magi who traveled from afar to bring gifts and to fall down in homage before the newborn incarnate Son of God (Matthew 2:10–11). These are the experiences, though unrecognized, of the guards in the passion scene in the Gospel of John who came to arrest Jesus but who fell on their faces when Jesus identified himself with the God of Moses in identifying himself with "I am" (John 18:4–6). In adoring God, we have no choice but to place our lives into the awesome, infinite, transcendent, and tender hands of God.

In summation, all these forms of prayer—every form of prayer—is a form of trust in and surrender to God in the different moments and circumstances of our lives. Our lives of prayer, then—and every occasion and moment of prayer—are an essential part of our daily, ongoing path of surrender with Jesus on the cross, and an empowerment to trust and surrender in those particularly difficult moments of our lives.

3. OUR RESPONSE TO THE UNIVERSAL CALL TO HOLINESS

The Second Vatican Council taught that every Christian, without exception, is called to holiness. Holiness is everyone's vocation; it is not the private reserve of priests, nuns, and hermits. We are all called to holiness—and nothing less. In fact, to desire less and to work for less than holiness is a tremendous act of ingratitude: Almighty God offers holiness to us—which means God calls us and empowers us—and how could sinful creatures refuse to take up such an amazing invitation?

Imagine how our lives would change if we really believed in this universal call as our own personal vocation! Imagine what kinds of lives we would lead if we took seriously the fact that holiness is our goal in this life, whatever our particular life circumstances. How would our lives change if we truly decided to take up this invitation and live it each day? How would priestly ministry, pastoral leadership, and parenting change if we took seriously the fact that enabling people to live authentically as Christian disciples means helping to walk the journey to holiness?

This understanding of our call and our goal helps us to understand the depth of prayer to which God is calling and inviting us.

Holiness means drawing close to God, becoming like God, being filled with the Spirit, entering into divine communion. Clearly it involves both a life of deepening prayer as well as good moral living, grounded increasingly in love that conforms us more and more to God's will and ways. While all of this may sound beyond the reach of most of our lives, we cannot let ourselves off the hook by shrugging our shoulders and leaving it to others to pursue this call. Holiness is, for all of us, a journey. Truly drawing close to God, becoming like God, opening oneself to the Spirit, entering into communion with God must, for most of us at least, begin simply and within the ordinary circumstances of our lives. We are not talking here about extraordinary phenomena like visions, ecstasies, or bilocating. Slowly, with the assistance of grace and dependent on the divine patience, we must set out and walk the journey of holiness, one day after another, more consistently and deeply, in prayer and right living in love.

In the end, of course, holiness is nothing less than the fulfillment of our humanity. We are most perfectly who and what we were meant to be when we are drawn close to and conformed to God. We do not reach such fulfillment overnight. It takes a lifetime of cooperating with God's grace in response to God's invitation. The path passes through our ordinary daily lives in our particular states in life. This fact does not make the path to holiness easy; but it helps us to see that it is possible.

We must believe that God wants the deepest possible communion with us, even in this life. And if that is true of what God wants for us, then it changes the sense of what our prayer should be like and to what it is directed. If it is true that our prayer must begin simply—and, in a sense, superficially with lots of talking on our parts—we cannot allow ourselves to be blind to the fact that God is always inviting and challenging us to grow deeper in prayer to an ever more intimate union with the divine.

Again, "deep" prayer does not equal holiness. Union with God—and authentic prayer—requires a more consistent and deeper conformity with love in concrete action and sustained attitude. Still, holiness requires deep prayer; and there is no doubt that such prayer requires time, discipline, and decision.

4. PARTICIPATION IN THE LIFE OF THE TRINITY

A fourth presupposition about prayer, very much related to holiness, is the fact that prayer is always a participation in the life of the triune God. Although Christian prayer is always centered on Christ and through Christ, there is no prayer to God that does not involve all three persons of the Trinity. This fact is evident in the sign of the cross that begins and ends many forms of liturgical, common prayer. It is evident in the form that liturgical prayer usually takes—addressed to the Father, through the Son, and in the Holy Spirit.

Through baptism, we are united with Christ. We are one with him. We were united with him in his saving action, going down with him into the tomb and rising up to new life as new creations when we were plunged in the baptismal waters and lifted up again. In our prayer, however simple, we are joined with Christ in his prayer. We are united with the eternal Son of God in the communion that he has shared with the Father in the Holy Spirit for all eternity. No doubt our union with Christ in prayer can and must grow deeper and more consistent, but this union characterizes all of our prayer. In that sense, all prayer is both a sharing in and an anticipation of our eternal participation in the very life of God.

Saint Paul tells us that it is the Spirit of God who helps in our prayer to express what we cannot speak on our own: "Likewise the Spirit helps us in our weakness; for we do not know how to pray as we ought, but that very Spirit intercedes with sighs too deep for words" (Romans 8:26). Baptized into Christ, we are always praying in the Spirit; and the Spirit, in union with our own spirit, prays from within us.

In summation, then, these four presuppositions about prayer have reminded us of four fundamental facts: Prayer is a response to the Good News of God's invitation to friendship with him. In prayer, we are always surrendering to God, in trusting as Jesus did and as we are called to do more broadly throughout our lives. In prayer, we are always responding to God's amazing invitation to draw close, to be conformed, to share the divine life—in short, to become holy. And, united in Christ, we are anticipating our share in the life of heaven as we open ourselves to the Spirit of God and are lifted into the life and heart of the triune God.

Growth in Prayer

Our discussion of prayer thus far makes it clear that in the matter of prayer, we must always be growing, moving forward, and deepening. The fact is that we can always respond to God more consistently and more deeply. We can always surrender in trust more completely as we follow Jesus to the cross of his total surrender. God's call to holiness is always calling us to more. The infinite life of the Trinity is always inviting us deeper.

In our tradition, it is expected that our prayer is meant to change, grow, and deepen. It is like growth in a friendship as we get to know each other more deeply. At first, there is a lot of talking, then there is increasing familiarity and comfort, then there is a greater ability to just be together, with a greater depth of knowledge, and finally we can be together without having to say anything. We can never be content with just saying the same prayers, doing the same things, unless we can also say that we find ourselves praying more deeply, more consistently, more "from the heart."

Such growth in prayer is meant to go hand-in-hand with a growth in love—with a greater love, lived out in action, for God and for neighbor. In fact, the two require each other. A true depth and consistency of love for God and neighbor requires a life of prayer; and such prayer can only grow in the fertile soil of a life and a heart growing in love.

Our prayer must grow from lots of talking at God...to quiet "being with" God; from occasional...to habitual; from when we feel like it...to always. For many of us, this last point is a critical lesson to learn. Just as love for God and neighbor is not principally a matter of warm feelings but rather of commitment and action, the same can be said of prayer. Especially perhaps in our world ruled by subjectivism, in which reality is judged by our felt reaction, we are tempted to judge our prayer by how it feels. We are tempted to think that our prayer is fine if it feels good, if we feel God's presence, if we feel better after our prayer. On the other hand, if we feel only dryness in prayer, if we find ourselves distracted, if we don't feel God's presence, we assume that we have done something wrong or that something is wrong with our prayer.

Our tradition tells us that we must judge our prayer, not by how it feels, but by the fruit it bears. If we can say that we seem to be growing more loving, more patient, more generous—that our commitment to follow Christ is growing firmer and more evident in action—then we can be sure that our prayer is sound and that we are opening ourselves to the works of the Spirit, regardless of how our prayer feels. As Saint Paul reminds us, "By contrast, the fruit of the Spirit is love, joy, peace, patience, kindness, generosity, faithfulness, gentleness, and self-control" (Galatians 5:22–23).

Certainly God does sometimes give us good feelings in prayer in order to attract us, to move us forward, to encourage us. But God's true movement within us occurs at a depth far beneath what we feel. And so, if we have good feelings in prayer...well, great. But if we depend on our feelings to determine our prayer, we will find ourselves only praying erratically. With such an elementary understanding of prayer, we will never develop a habit of prayer nor will we grow in prayer.

We must remember that, ultimately, prayer is about surrender and trust. It is not about how we feel. Even at a purely human level, strong relationships do not develop if we spend time together only when we feel like it or only when we're "getting something out of it" at any particular moment.

In the end, prayer is an essential part of our decision to be

Christian. It is a response to God's prior invitation, but it is also a decision and a commitment on our part. A life of sustained prayer, day in and day out, when we feel like it and when we don't, is a necessary part of our fundamental life choice for God in answer to the divine call and invitation. And, in turn, our prayer helps to shape and strengthen our freedom to say "yes" to God in our daily lives.

For all of us, the decision for and commitment to prayer requires a decision to make time for this conversation with God, to fit it into our busy lives and commit ourselves to it. As we all know, we can almost always manage to make time for what is important to us. One of my brother monks used to say that if you're too busy to pray, you're just too busy. If we have truly decided to be Christian, we will make time for prayer, and we will strive to make our prayer always deeper.

Questions for Reflection

* *How would you personally define prayer? How would you explain it to an unchurched friend?*

* *What might God be asking you to surrender in your life at this moment?*

* *Have you experienced a call to go deeper in prayer? How has your prayer changed, grown, deepened over the years?*

* *What helps you to support, strengthen, or maintain your prayer? What would you advise a beginner or someone struggling to grow in prayer?*

* *Have you seen your prayer "bear fruit" in particular ways in your life?*

* *How would you like to see your prayer grow? What seems to you to be the next step? What would have to happen or change?*

Prayer

How can it be, O God of the universe, all holy, all God, all powerful, that you call this sinner into communion with you, that you desire holy converse with the merest creature? And yet, in faith, I know that it is so. More and more, in prayer and in daily living, guide me in the ways of communion with you, with your holy will, with your loving ways. Bring me more profoundly into your divine heart, O triune God, so that I may truly love as you have loved for all eternity. Through Christ our Lord. Amen.

10

IN THE COMMUNION
OF THE SAINTS

At first glance, it might seem that the closer we grow to God and the more intimate our relationship is, the more that our lives would become focused on this divine relationship to the exclusion of others. It is true that the experience of deep prayer invites us to a more intense solitude and silence so that we can be alone with God. However, it would be wrong to think that deep prayer reduces our sense of connection with and concern for others. In fact, the closer we draw to God, the more apparent the depth of our relationship with others becomes. While the hermit may have very limited contact with other persons, this does not mean that he or she is less aware of or in touch with the reality of relationships with other human beings. In fact, this awareness can be intensified.

When we encounter and draw close to God, we find more profoundly that God is holding all people in existence, as God does for each one of us, holding us all together in the divine heart. In fact, it is in God that we can truly discover the fundamental depth of our inherent relationship with others.

We have been created in the image of God, who is a communion of love. In the heart of God is an eternal relation of love between and among the three persons of the Trinity. Created in the image of this God, we are created to be in relationship with others, in this life and in the life to come. We are created to be in relationships of mutual self-giving with the persons of the blessed Trinity—Holy Spirit, Son, and Father. This is who we are and what we are meant to be. Authentically drawing close to God does not draw us away from others. On the contrary, drawing close to God enables us to see more clearly that we are in relationship with others and that our fulfillment and destiny can be found precisely in this communion with others in God.

The Scriptures reveal to us that God has always called men and women together into community. One of the most fundamental themes of the Hebrew Scriptures is covenant, the community into which God calls the people and with which God binds himself. And, through the prophets, God challenges the people to be attentive to the people at the edges of the covenant—widows, orphans, the poor—people who are at the edges because of human action contrary to the covenant, not because of the divine will and action. Building on the faith of Israel, Jesus also called people together, reaching out to the margins, to the poor, the sinner, the outcast. But more, Jesus reached out beyond the strict bounds of the old covenant and extended his mission to the gentiles. After he rose from the dead, he commanded the disciples to continue his mission to the ends of the earth.

The Christian life is fundamentally a communal life, a life with and for others. We are baptized into a community of disciples, a living communion: the body of Christ of which we are all members. We receive the gift of faith from a community with a shared history, gathered and guided by the Spirit. At its best, the Christian community is a communion of brothers and sisters who support, help, nurture, encourage, and challenge one another as together they seek to gather all into the body of Christ. Our communal worship is most profound at the eucharistic feast where Christ gathers his people through the Holy Spirit and makes himself present.

Further, the images that Jesus uses to describe the world to come are clearly communal images, notably for example, the heavenly banquet. The Book of Revelation sees a future in which the elect of God will stand together around the throne of God.

Relationship with others is at the heart of who we are as human beings. It is at the heart, too, of what we are called to be and to live. It is our destiny.

It is critical for us to keep our eyes focused on this fundamental Christian truth. In an often individualistic Western society, our temptation is to focus our attention on our own personal fulfillment and our individual relationship with God. This is to the detriment of a continued growth in faith and Christian living for those who share in the life of the body of Christ. While we have a personal relationship with God, it is not a private relationship in the sense that others are excluded or beyond our scope of concern. The Christian life and prayer cannot be reduced to our private, individual project of self-fulfillment.

Moreover, sin is always trying to draw us into an attitude of narrow self-concern, whether that sin is the selfishness that exists in our heart or as it has become embodied in the priorities, structures, and ways of relating in the world around us. Sin is a "no" to God and to neighbor, a refusal of love and a refusal to love. It always has an essentially selfish character. This kind of me-first attitude to the exclusion of active interest and concern for others becomes embedded in the world around us. We see it lived in the ways that people do or don't relate to one another. Thus we can be blinded little by little to the actual demands of loving God and neighbor, and we then contribute further to this blindness through our own acts of selfishness.

There are people today who say, "I believe in God, I just don't believe in institutional religion," or, "I don't believe that you have to belong to a church in order to pray to God." To the degree that statements like these are a critique of an overemphasis on institutional structures to the detriment of people, faith, and relationship within a community of faith, or an affirmation that God listens to our personal prayers wherever we might be, well, fair enough. But the fact remains that there is no authentic Christian faith, Christian discipleship, or way of life apart from belonging to Christ's body, the living, historical community of his disciples.

Even regarding the Church as an institution, with its established structures, procedures, and law, the fact is that we are by nature human, embodied in physical human flesh and limited. We cannot have sustained community without such realities. While the Church transcends earthly realities, it remains at the same time a human institution. And, as Catholics, we believe that it is the very will of Jesus and the fruit of the Holy Spirit's guidance that the community of faith should have established and trusted teachers and shepherds. Yes, it is true that, at its heart, the Church is a community, a communion of word and sacrament. But the sustained life of this community requires the support of institutional structures and relationships.

Spiritually, we certainly have our own personal prayer and relationship with God. However, prayer is never really completely private or individual. To the degree that we are truly praying in the Holy Spirit, our prayer is united with the prayer of every other believer, whether consciously or not. In the same way, morally, we must make our own adult decisions based on our well-formed consciences. But our consciences cannot be authentically formed outside the wisdom of the Christian community, its moral teaching, and its Spirit-guided teachers. We cannot act rightly without considering the impact of our actions on others. On the other hand, we must see that our sin, even what appears to be the most private and unseen, impacts others, if for no other reason than we thereby make ourselves less an instrument and channel of God's gracious presence in our lives.

The Eucharist is our great teacher, the great school of Christian living where we come to know Christ and abide in his love. At the Eucharist, Christ gathers together his people to celebrate our shared faith in the Good News. We come together as brothers and sisters, no matter our gender, economic state, race, or ethnic and cultural background. We worship as one people, and together we share in the one Body and the one Blood, in holy Communion with God in Christ and with one another.

But more, we believe that, at the Eucharist, we commune not only with people we see around us. In Christ, in his body, we commune as well with people of faith throughout the world, with faithful Christians who have gone before us, with the saints in heaven—with all of those who, with us, have chosen to follow Christ. We depend on one another to sustain and deepen that commitment. In the Eucharist, our true, fundamental, and expansive relationship with others becomes apparent, real, and celebrated. And so, too, does our responsibility to participate actively and to build up and contribute to the life of the community of faith.

And again, as the Eucharist reveals our communion with one another in faith and in love, the sacrament of reconciliation reveals that we tragically share in the reality of sin, that our sin impacts others and contributes to the presence of sin around us. As a result, we need to appeal both to God and to our brothers and sisters for pardon and assistance—as we do, for example, in the *Confiteor* of the Mass: "I confess to almighty God and to you, my brothers and sisters...."

As Catholics, we have a distinctive belief in our relationship with those who have gone before us, that is, with the communion of saints. The saints are not distant, unrelated, and disconnected historical figures. They are friends, guides, and intercessors for us in heaven, and this truth is the heart of our traditional Catholic devotion to saints. The feast days of saints that mark our liturgical calendar and the statues of saints in our churches and homes remind us of all of the saints who surround us at every moment. We pray to the saints as friends, asking for help. However, unlike the friends we see around us, the saints do not pray for us outside of God's purposes and plans. Rather, they live in full communion with God and thus are already united with God's loving will for us and those we love. These heavenly friends join their prayers to ours for our true good and the good of those we love.

The greatest saint is the Blessed Virgin Mary. Devotion to her as witness, example, and preeminently united with God in her Son is an important element of Catholic faith and spirituality. The Mother of Jesus, she is also Mother of his body, the Church, and the Mother of every Christian. She is the first disciple. Although the Gospels tell us very little about the life of Mary, every story that it tells of her is clear testimony that she is the true follower of Christ and a worthy example to us all—whether in her decisive "yes" to the angel at the annunciation or her silent acquiescence to God's will at the foot of the cross.

The communion of saints calls to mind once again the shared destiny that is God's intention for us, as well as the divine invitation offered to us. In this life, we strive to love God and neighbor, to pray with and for others, to participate actively in the life of the Church as an anticipation, foretaste, and participation in that communal life to come. Our personal decision to follow Jesus only makes sense in this shared context. Our freedom can only be nourished and grow within the community of believers. Our prayerful surrender into communion with God is at the same time true communion with all the saints.

Questions for Reflection

* *How is the Christian community important for your life of and growth in faith?*

* *How do you contribute to the life of your local community of faith?*

* *Do you have a devotion to a particular saint(s)? Why? Has it changed over time? How does this devotion support your life as a Christian?*

* *How can you grow in a deeper attention and devotion to the Eucharist and a deeper sense of the presence of the saints joining you in celebration at the eucharistic feast?*

Prayer

God of heaven and earth, of the saints in heaven, and of the living here below, Christ Jesus has graciously brought me in to the life of his body, the Church. Let me draw life from my sharing in this great, living communion and, in my small way, let me contribute to its being built up. Let your holy saints and most especially the Queen of Heaven inspire me and pray for me so that I may live more authentically each day the discipleship to which I have been so mercifully called by Jesus Christ, the head of the Church, in whose gracious name I pray. Amen.

11

THE LIFE BEYOND

The Christian journey is a life lived in hope. Hope is the abiding attitude, the disposition, to look ahead to the future with expectation—in Christian terms, to look ahead to a future at this moment not clear to our normal vision, when God will fulfill the divine promises made to us and to all God's people. In moments of difficulty, Christian faith gives us the ability to see already, with the vision of faith, the good that God will bring from current struggle, though at this moment it might be impossible to see how this could be. In Christian hope, we look forward to the eternal life that God has promised us.

As we have seen before, so much of a true understanding of the Christian life depends on a clear sense of our creation in the image of God—for example, our inherent relationship with others and our perfection in love. In a similar way, we come to a true understanding of the meaning of Christian discipleship by looking to the eternal destiny that God has planned for us. Let's look at how our belief in heaven, hell, and purgatory reveal the shape and demands of our daily living as Christians.

The Life Beyond

HEAVEN

Popularly, we think of heaven as a place we go after death if we have lived a good life. There, we will enjoy a vision of God, seeing God face to face. If our imagining of heaven is more ample, we see that Jesus' image of the eternal banquet of heaven suggests a vision of heaven as our shared enjoyment of communion with God. Created in the image of a relational triune God of love, we are called to love and be concerned for others in this life as an anticipation and promise of the shared communion of heaven.

But the Christian belief in heaven really points to something still more profound and reveals other deep truths of our Christian life. Heaven is not so much a place where we will see God, as if we were going to live for all eternity gazing at God from outside. In heaven, we will live forever in the heart of God. United with Christ in baptism, we will receive the love poured out by the Father on the Son for all eternity as a love poured out on us personally and on all of us together made one in Christ. And from our hearts will well up the love that the Son has returned to the Father for all eternity and the word of love spoken by the Son for all ages: "*Abba*, our Father." And so we will be filled with the Holy Spirit as the love that has flowed eternally between the Father and the Son. Heaven is to live in the heart of the eternal triune God forever.

We are forming our freedom in this life precisely so we can say "yes" to God for all eternity. We are seeking to conform our lives to God's will now so we can be conformed to God forever. We seek to give ourselves in love freely and selflessly in this life in anticipation and as preparation to give and to receive the divine love of heaven.

In our belief in heaven, we see again how love is our perfection and our destiny. As Christians, we believe that we were created to share in a great communion with others in the heart of God. In heaven, we will meet all of those who have said "yes" to God in this life. This communal vision of heaven also reveals the deeper reality of prayer. In prayer, we don't just talk to God nor do we just raise our hearts and minds to God. In all true prayer, we open ourselves to the Holy Spirit. And in the Spirit, we commune with the triune God in anticipation of that full communion of heaven. Yes, our communion can and should grow far deeper, more intimate, more abiding than it is. But each moment of prayer, however we might experience it, is a realization of this communion at some level, so long as our heart is open and our will desires it. How much more deeply, too, we must understand our communion with Christ at the Eucharist as a sharing in him with the triune life of God!

HELL

The Christian belief in hell also reveals the deeper reality of living the Christian life in the present. As we have seen, in this life, freedom's truest purpose is our "yes" to God. This must be the fundamental direction of our lives, a fundamental life choice that shapes all of our individual choices. Sin is a refusal, a "no" to God's invitation to life and communion, and so a denial of our truest purpose and meaning. God created us with freedom to say "yes" to him, and Jesus died and rose to set us free from the power of sin so that we could respond to the divine invitation as we were made to do.

If, in our daily lives, we have made a habit of saying "no" to God, if we have fundamentally refused God's love and invitation in some serious way, when the veil is lifted and we see God face to face, we will find that we are unable to say "yes" to the divine self-offering. In the instant we see God—who is infinite love, beauty, and truth—we will see that we were made for God and for communion with God. But we will be unable to speak the "yes" that we were created and redeemed to say. This is the moment of judgment. It is the gateway to hell. It is not so much the just wrath of a God who has coldly calculated our every failing and carefully balanced the good and bad in our lives, it is rather the consequence of our own fundamental life decision, commitment, and stance.

In a real sense, in every decision we are making ourselves to be a certain way; we are constructing an identity. In every true decision, in every manifestation of our human freedom, we decide for ourselves the kind of people we will be. And we decide for ourselves what our stance will be toward God. It is true that not every decision is life-changing and fundamentally decisive. But by the same token, it is true that we cannot freely perform an action, for good or ill, and think that it does not make us be a certain kind of person or that it is not a response to God's invitation to enter into divine communion. I cannot speak falsehoods to people who have a right to the truth and, at the same time, think that this does not make me a liar. Nor can I think that my lie has no relation to God, who is truth and the author of all truth. If I think of myself as an honest person, while being in the habit of telling lies, I am simply self-deceived because, in fact, I am dishonest, a liar. On the other hand, by my good actions and acts of love, I make myself to be a good person and respond to God and to the divine invitation.

How utterly essential it is to say "yes" to God in this life and in every choice. How necessary it is to claim the freedom that God has given us and that Christ has won for us, to deepen and to shape it. This "yes" is our purpose, our task, our hope for an eternal future with the triune God. And it is a "yes" that must be spoken implicitly in every decision we make.

PURGATORY

The Catholic doctrine of purgatory reflects our belief that our graced work of conversion doesn't end at death. In fact, it intensifies the purgation, the asceticism, that should mark our present living as Christians and thereby sheds light on our daily and lifelong challenge. When we pass from this life, when we see God in unimaginable divine goodness and love, at that very instant we will also see ourselves as we truly are. The object that may have looked nearly flawless in the half-darkness, when brought into the full light, reveals every flaw, every blemish, every crack. In the light of that infinite love, we will see the depths of our lovelessness, our true capacity for selfishness, the hideous specter of our history of sin. In the light of God's infinitely superabundant mercy, we will see how small our hearts have been, how slow to forgive, how petty our concerns. In the light of God's generosity, we will be forced to confront our greed and covetousness; in the light of the divine fidelity and constancy, our fickleness; in light of God's justice, our halfhearted concern for the needs and the rights of others.

At that moment in which we will see both the infinitely good God and ourselves as we are, how terrible will be the revelation of our sin. How deep the shame and regret, how profound the repentance—and, at the very same time, how awesome and certain the vision of God's unfailing mercy, the outstretched hand, the voice inviting us into the eternal divine embrace. And, because our "yes" to God in this life has not been as deep and consistent as it ought to have been, we will embrace the purgation, the burning away of all that is not of God, that we did not accomplish in this life—a purifying both terrible and sweet—until our "yes" to God can be made pure and all-encompassing: purgatory.

This teaching about purgatory calls us to attend, with a mighty seriousness, to the work of making our "yes" to God in this life more consistent, deeper, more complete—by refraining from sin, uprooting sin's hold in the depth of our hearts and minds, strengthening and shaping our freedom, growing in virtue and in love, and by a growing consistency, depth, and intimacy in prayer. All of this, not so much out of fear of hell or the desire to avoid purgatory, but out of a humble gratitude and grateful love for the invitation and promise of eternal communion with and in the heart of the triune God.

As we have seen, the closer we grow to God, the more we see our sin. But, drawn close to God, the greater clarity of our sin reveals yet more clearly the unimaginable, undeserved mercy of God. And, in humble gratitude, we find yet renewed reason to grow in the depth and lived reality of our decision to be Christian.

Questions for Reflection

* *Do you think much about life after death? How have you imagined it to be?*

* *Does the thought of the future life inspire you in your daily living? If so, how?*

* *Do you find it helpful to think about the suffering of hell?*

* *Are you a person of hope? Have you ever failed in hope?*

* *How are you or can you be a messenger of hope to others in your life?*

Prayer

Timeless God of time and infinity, joy of the blessed in heaven, and hope of all your faith-filled people, let the promise of your heavenly dwelling places inspire me each day to live the Christian faith with which you have gifted me. Cleanse me now, purge me of all sin, root out sin's death-dealing roots in me that I may not be delayed in entering into the divine communion which, undeserving, I am invited by your infinite and tender love. Give me a holy resolve in the face of whatever stands in my way and a firm hope in the face of any obstacle that I find within me or without, until at last I share eternal life in the heart of Father, Son, and Spirit. In the name of Christ Jesus, whose name I so undeservedly bear. Amen.

"GIVE TO GOD WHAT IS GOD'S"

The Gospels tell us that the Pharisees tried to entrap Jesus by asking him if the Jews had to pay taxes to their hated Roman occupiers (Matthew 22:15–22; Mark 12:13–17; Luke 20:20–26). Jesus simply asked to see a coin and said: "Whose head [image] is this, and whose title?" When they replied that it was the emperor's, Jesus responded famously: "Give therefore to the emperor the things that are the emperor's, and to God the things that are God's."

This text has traditionally been a tool to try to understand the sometimes complex loyalties of Christians living in the world, including the particular question of the involvement of Christians in the world of politics in a democratic society. And appropriately so. Given both the context of the story and the words of Jesus to "give to Caesar what is Caesar's," the story provides guidance to consider those important and thorny sorts of questions.

At the same time, we can't neglect the second part of what Jesus said in this Gospel story: "give to God the things that are God's." The Roman coin bore the image of the emperor, and so it should be given to him. But what of us, who bear the image of God?

Give to God What Is God's

We must give to God what is God's. God has created us in the divine image; and in the previous chapters we have had the opportunity to examine several layers of what this means for living an authentic human life. As we have seen, because we are created in the divine image, our fulfillment as human beings will be found in conforming our lives to God's loving will, in drawing close and participating in the divine life. We must do so by choice, by decision, and by commitment, made possible by God's gracious action. We must give to God what is God's—which is to say, our very lives, each in our own circumstances. Only in that way will we be truly what we are meant to be.

At the very beginning of the rite of infant baptism, the minister addresses the infant in the name of the Church: "I claim you for Christ our Savior by the sign of the cross"; and then the minister makes the sign of the cross on the forehead of the child. Each one of us, then, has been "claimed for Christ"; and each of us has been marked—"branded," if you will—with the symbol of our true master. We are Christ's, and Christ is God's (1 Corinthians 3:23). And so, we must choose to live according to the reality of whose we are.

The Bible tells us that our God is a jealous God (Exodus 20:5; 34:14), which is to say that our God wants it all: no other gods. God has created us out of pure love, without our deserving, and offers us a share in the divine life itself. God has offered us everything, and we cannot be satisfied unless we freely take up this wondrous invitation. God is infinite. God has created us with an infinite capacity for the divine self-gift. God has invited us to share the infinite divine life. And so, there is an unavoidable totality in the decision and commitment that we must make.

But more, the fact is that, in Jesus, God has given all to us. The Father has given his only begotten Son to and for us. God has given all, and God invites us to give all in return. Of course, this is what it means to share in the life of the triune God: to receive the Father's eternal self-giving to the Son and, with the Son, to give ourselves completely in return.

Again, the totality God requires is not restricted to a special group of Christians. Yes, the Christian commitment takes particular form within particular states of life, but the fundamental commitment and demands are the same for all. It is the ordinary Christian commitment and nothing less: participation in the life of the Church, the life of deepening prayer, loving service of others, and embracing and carrying the cross as we experience it in our own unique way. Married Christians, for example, live this invitation distinctively within the context of their relationship, in their own self-giving to one another in sacramental marriage. In this way, the couple gives witness to the relationship between Christ and the Church (Ephesians 5:25–33). Neither husband nor wife are diminished in this relationship of love. Each remains an individual, but they are each fulfilled in their self-giving within their vocation.

In Jesus, God gives all; and, united with Christ through baptism, we must give all. This truth is celebrated again in every Eucharist. In the Eucharist, we share in the Body and Blood of Christ, offered to and for us, once for all, on the cross. Christ gives himself completely to us in our communion. And, in return, we offer ourselves with him to the Father, by uniting ourselves with Christ's all sufficient sacrifice.

"You shall love the Lord your God with all your heart, and with all your soul, and with all your mind..." and "...You shall love your neighbor as yourself" (Matthew 22:37–39). We all know those words. At one level, we all accept them. But we also have to accept that Jesus really means what he says. And then we have to set out to live the challenge he has given us.

We Must Decide to Be Christian

To be truly Christian is to set out to follow Jesus along the way that leads to the cross and ultimately through the resurrection to participation in the divine life of the Trinity. This is what God offers us in Christ. We must decide and commit ourselves to accept and to live that commitment faithfully and ever more authentically.

We must decide to be Christian. In any age, it is easier said than done, each day and for a lifetime. Our world today presents its unique challenges. But in order to truly live a decision to be Christian, and thus to love God and neighbor with the selfless totality to which we are called, we must be free. We must be free, not in some superficial sense, but truly and deeply free to give ourselves freely and generously in love. This is the great challenge and task of our daily lives as Christians, and it is unavoidably linked with the challenge of Jesus to take up the cross and follow him. The cross of suffering, the cross of ascetical practice, the cross of accepting life's realities, the cross of the demands of prayer, the cross of a "dark faith"—this is the path by which the freedom that Christ has won for us is made a reality.

We must decide to be Christian, and, with the help of grace, we must daily engage the challenge of growing in the freedom to live that most fundamental Christian commitment.

Questions for Reflection

* *What are you holding back from God at this moment?*

* *Why are you a Christian today?*

* *What would you say to a friend who was wavering in the practice of his or her faith?*

* *What do you need to do now to make your Christian commitment stronger?*

Prayer

Bountiful God, in your infinite, merciful love, you have given me everything in Jesus, who shared my human flesh and died and rose for me and for all. What I can give you in return is the merest pittance in light of what you have so miraculously poured out on me and on all the world. But, in faith, I believe that your love wants from me the feeble love that I have to give you in return. Let me give it then wholeheartedly. Let me not hold back. Let me give you what is really yours: my praise, my thanksgiving, my life, my love. In Jesus' name I pray. Amen.